The Gift of Administration

New Testament Foundations for the Vocation of Administrative Service

Donald Senior, CP

LITURGICAL PRESS
Collegeville, Minnesota

www.litpress.org

2   3   4   5   6   7   8   9

Library of Congress Cataloging-in-Publication Data

Senior, Donald.

The gift of administration : New Testament foundations for the vocation of administrative service / Donald Senior, C.P.

    pages   cm

    Includes bibliographical references and index.

    ISBN 978-0-8146-4716-5 — ISBN 978-0-8146-4741-7 (ebook)

    1. Church management.   2. Vocation—Christianity.   I. Title.

BV652.S43   2016

254—dc23   2015028797

"Donald Senior brings together in this volume a wealth of personal and professional experience: extensive theological study, research, writing, and teaching, along with twenty-three years as president of a graduate school of theology. He provides a cogent scriptural foundation for understanding the work of administration as both a calling and a gift and does so in ways that are inviting, inspiring, and encouraging. Senior's stirring words find genuine and profound meaning in everything from fund-raising to finances. This is a must-read for all who are called to serve as administrators."

> —Abbot Gregory Polan, OSB
> Conception Abbey
> Conception Seminary College

"The author of *The Gift of Administration* holds the unusual credentials of a renowned biblical scholar and a skilled, admired administrator. The book reflects the gifts of both vocations as Donald Senior fittingly brings to bear the biblical imperatives that require leaders to serve without seeking honors. In a central chapter on the responsibility of building community, he identifies many qualities of a truly spiritual leader, such as one who is courageous, compassionate, humble, truthful, and understanding. Throughout the book, those looking for practical applications will find them in chapters on mission and planning, finances and fund-raising, among many others."

> —Sister Katarina Schuth, OSF
> Endowed Chair for the Social Scientific Study of Religion
> St. Paul Seminary School of Divinity
> University of St. Thomas

"Father Donald Senior's latest work combines sound exegesis with astute reflections that are the fruit of a long and successful career in higher education administration. In identifying the various activities of the administrator—articulating the mission, leading, planning, fund-raising, communicating—as expressions of discipleship that are founded in the New Testament itself, Father Senior has uncovered a hitherto neglected theological and spiritual depth of administration. And, as we have come to expect from Father Senior, he writes with clarity and precision. This book should be required reading for bishops, pastors, mission leaders, educational administrators, or anyone else who has responded to the call to be a steward of the church's goods."

> —Rev. Seán Charles Martin
> President
> Aquinas Institute of Theology

"In this book, Father Senior provides a firm biblical foundation for the charism of 'steering' the barque of Christ—flowing from the call of Jesus who laid out the vision of the servant leader. The Church on mission needs servants good at planning, coordination, and communication. Father Senior contributes to a ministry easily taken for granted."

> —Most Reverend Joseph E. Kurtz, DD
> Archbishop of Louisville
> President, United States Conference of Catholic Bishops

"*The Gift of Administration* is itself a gift to leaders of religious institutions. Donald Senior is as able a New Testament scholar as he is an administrative leader, and he connects administration in the present moment with patterns of churchly leadership described in the New Testament. The result is true wisdom from the long tradition in a field dominated by advice from present experience. *The Gift of Administration* is simply the best book I have ever read on administrative leadership; it stands high above a crowded field of contenders."

> —Daniel Aleshire
> Executive Director
> Association of Theological Schools in the United States and Canada

"With equal parts erudition and inspiration in his remarkable book, *The Gift of Administration*, Donald Senior reframes the necessary work of administration as life-giving ministry. Grounded in Scripture and rich theological tradition, this book will surely inform and encourage all who are entrusted with the leadership and management of faith-based organizations."

> —Kerry Alys Robinson
> Executive Director
> National Leadership Roundtable on Church Management

"The time was long overdue for a biblical and theological book about administrative work. The beauty of *The Gift of Administration* is that Senior not only draws rich material from Scripture but also provides indispensable frames from different theologians and leaders like Dietrich Bonhoeffer and Pope Francis for approaching the role of administrator. This is a unique and invaluable resource."

> —Rick Bliese
> President
> In Trust Center for Theological Schools

Contents

Preface

The impulse to write this book comes from the strange blend of responsibilities that I have been engaged in over the past several years. Shortly before my ordination as a priest, my superiors asked me to pursue graduate biblical studies at Louvain University in Belgium. Prior to that assignment, I had dreamed of being an overseas missionary once I was ordained. I remember being deeply moved by the report of one of our Passionist missionaries in Korea who described his experience on the Island of Sorokdo, ministering to the lepers who were confined there. Boyhood memories of stories about the heroic Saint Damian of Molokai, the Belgian missionary who had served the lepers and himself had contracted the disease, came rushing back. Who could forget the drama of his revealing that he had contracted the disease by addressing his congregation at Sunday Mass with the words, "We lepers . . ."

But like an arranged marriage, my superiors had another proposal in mind. And, as I understand can happen with arranged marriages, I fell in love with my new destiny. I had had two great biblical professors in my seminary days—Barnabas Ahern and Carroll Stuhlmueller—both of whom were at the forefront of the resurgent biblical movement in Catholicism and both of whom imbued a deep love for the Scriptures in their students. So after my ordination in 1967, I went off to the University of Louvain and earned a doctorate in theology and Sacred Scripture under the fearsome tutelage of a truly great scholar, the late Frans Neirynck. He was a resolute task-master, but because of him, I learned what scholarship with rigor and integrity meant, and that experience has guided me in my own work ever since.

In 1972, at the completion of my doctoral work, I returned to the United States and took up teaching at the newly formed Catholic Theological Union in Chicago, a graduate school of theology sponsored by several religious communities. For the first sixteen years of my time on CTU's faculty, I reveled in the work of teaching and writing in the field of New Testament. CTU encouraged its faculty to offer service to the wider Church, so I was also busy with lectures and workshops across the country and involvement in a number of publications on biblical topics.

In 1987 my world shifted unexpectedly. Our president at the time resigned abruptly, worn down by his duties. I was in Australia when this happened, giving a series of lectures during the first (and only) academic sabbatical of my career, but the phone call of the chair of our board reached across the Pacific early one morning and asked me if I would consider becoming acting president while the search for a new president was underway. The year before, I had served as acting dean for CTU—but with the proviso that I would not be a candidate for the permanent position. Having completed that task—and having escaped being elected dean—I was a prime target to be acting president. I agreed, but again with the proviso that I would not be a candidate for president. I loved teaching and thought that my whole training and preparation would be wasted if I moved into full-time administration.

As fate—or Providence?—would have it, the search for a new president came up empty and the board turned to me to accept the role. After pondering for a while and consulting my religious superior, I agreed to make the jump into what for me was an entirely new role. I had served as a program director, a department head, and as acting dean, but in these roles my administrative duties were either part time or, in the case of acting dean, transitory. Now I was into administration with both feet!

After eight years in the role of president, I thought I had paid my dues and happily returned to my work teaching on the CTU faculty. But not for long—my successor was a wonderful, warm, and kind human being, an exemplary priest. Because of a number of factors, however, he found the work of president overwhelming and graciously agreed to step down after only a year and a half on the job. Worried about the institution appearing to its publics as unstable, the Board of Trustees urged me to return as president. I did so, but not as a heroic sacrifice, even though I had been very happy after leaving the president's office to return to teaching full-time. In fact, I had experienced great satisfaction in my first stint as president. The work of administration opened me up to experiences and learning that I realized I would never have acquired in my role as a faculty member—as sacred and fulfilling as that role had been for me. Suddenly I found myself working with accomplished laymen and women on our Board of Trustees, encountering leaders in the civic, professional, and business world of Chicago in seeking their support for the mission of CTU, interacting with Church leaders in Chicago, the United States, and even the Vatican, and working with and surely learning from a whole new cadre of colleagues who served as presidents and deans of great Protestant schools of theology through involvement in the Association of Theological

Schools of the United States and Canada. All of these contacts with remarkable people were like a new school of life for me, opening my eyes to realities that previously I hardly knew.

Thus returning to full-time administration after a brief respite was not a terrible burden, even though I had not sought it. I had, unexpectedly, a great deal of satisfaction in my first turn at being president. Likewise, I had freely left the office in the first place after a decent length of time. Being urged to come back gave me a sense of freedom and serenity in returning to this role. My CTU colleagues knew I was not motivated by an unquenchable desire to be president, and I was acting freely and for the good of the school. I continued to serve as president for another sixteen years. Combined with my first stint, I was privileged to serve as president of CTU for twenty-three years, finally stepping down in June 2013.

All during that time, I thought it was important that I maintain as best I could my involvement in biblical scholarship. I taught some courses each year, especially in our sabbatical program and summer institute, offered workshops and study days for the wider Church, and continued to write and edit in both popular and technical journals. In 2002, I was appointed by Pope John Paul II to the Pontifical Biblical Commission. I served three popes (John Paul II, Benedict XVI, and Francis) in the course of my terms on this commission, and this work, too, helped keep me abreast of biblical scholarship in a unique way. I found that all of this academic work of teaching and writing was not a hindrance to my responsibilities as president but actually helped me maintain my involvement in the life of the school.

It is this blend of biblical studies and administrative experience that led me to this book. Over time I came to see both biblical scholarship and the work of administration as expressions of my vocation as a Christian. Both, I was convinced, were deeply rooted in the nature of the Gospel and the mission entrusted to the Church by the Risen Christ. But, while it was easy to see the connection between my faith as a Christian and the vocation of studying and teaching the Scriptures, it took me some time to appreciate the fact that administration, too, was an authentic, Gospel-rooted ministry. For many, both in the academy and in the Church, administrative work is viewed as a "necessary evil," as something that somebody has to do in order to keep the lights on and the doors open but only ancillary to the real mission of a school of theology—or a parish or any other religious institution. Like flossing one's teeth, it was a required duty but not what gave meaning to one's day.

Sometimes I experienced that this view of administration, which is often unstated but nevertheless present, can lead colleagues who have other roles in a Christian institution to look down on those in administration. On the occasion of my first being elected as president, one of my colleagues and friends on the faculty, said "better you than me" in a tone that suggested I had contracted some disease or fallen into some terrible misfortune! Teaching and counseling and preaching and leading worship are, it seemed, the true works of ministry; doing administrative tasks was considered second class. In my experience, when major administrative posts came open in our school and in other schools I was familiar with, there were not lines of candidates clamoring for the jobs.

What I hope to accomplish in this book is to draw on my blend of background in both biblical studies and administrative service to show how the work of administration is truly a work of ministry. I write not as a theorist about management but as a practitioner of administration in a religious institution. The overall purpose of administration and its defining tasks all have a strong base in the Scriptures and in Christian tradition. Exposure to this book may not transform reluctant stewards into enthusiastic administrators nor cause crowds of candidates to seek administrative work in religious institutions. But hopefully it will demonstrate that, as Paul the apostle noted, administration is one of the gifts the Risen Christ gives to his Church (1 Cor 12:28) and thereby help those involved in this ministry to realize that serving as an administrator is an authentic expression of the Church's mission in the world. Hence the title of this book.

My experience as an administrator has been in Catholic institutions, although I had the privilege of serving as president of the Association of Theological Schools in the United States and Canada and being a member of its board for several years—an experience of governance in an ecumenical setting that I cherish. I hope that what I offer in this book will be of use not only to Catholic administrators but also to all Christians who are involved in administrative service.

Sitting down to write this book brought to memory the many friends, colleagues, and mentors who taught me how to do my job. I thought of the superb trustees I worked with, many of whom became personal friends and I often felt part of their families—celebrating baptisms and weddings and funerals—which was always a privilege. I think of the board chairs who in a particular way supported and directed me: Michael Higgins, CP, the late Anthony O'Connell, OSM, the late Marty Kirk, CMF, Tom Reynolds, SSC, Michael Slattery, OSA, and Kurt Hartrich, OFM. I was also privileged to serve closely with some outstanding academic deans: Tom McGonigle, OP, Kathleen Hughes, RSCJ, Gary Riebe-Estrella, SVD, and Barbara Reid, OP. A president soon learns that partnership with your finance officer is crucial; I was fortunate to serve with excellent partners: Maureen Meter, Bernice Frederick, and Mike Connors. For me, the president has to work hand in glove with your development officer. I will always be grateful to Cy Maus who helped me get our development program off the ground, to his successor Emily John, to Bill Booth—who guided us through our first capital campaigns—and to Anne Marie Tirpak who helped lift our program to a whole new level. Getting the word out in an effective and appropriate way depends on good public relations and communications people. I was blessed to have excellent ones in Regina Baiocchi, Pattie Sporrong Thompson, Stephanie Sinnott Boland, Beth White, and Nancy Nickel. Hardly least, excellent personal assistants kept me on track these past years: Shirley Brin, Margaret Cassidy, Valerie Holloway, and Pam Pauloski, SP. I can't thank them enough.

As I mentioned above, a special blessing for me was to be engaged with the Association of Theological Schools of the United States and Canada all during the time I served as president of CTU. This ecumenical organization is both a fully licensed accrediting agency and a professional support organization that has been instrumental in providing on the job training for a host of theological educators and administrators. I especially appreciate my association with its superb executive director Dan Aleshire and with fellow board chairs who became friends and heroes to me as I learned the ropes: Martha Horne, David Tiede, Cynthia Campbell, John Kinney, Richard Mouw, and J. Dorcas Gordan.

I was blessed to serve as president of CTU during the tenure of two great archbishops of Chicago, Joseph Cardinal Bernardin and Francis Cardinal George. Each of them was a great support and inspiration to me and understood well the mission of a school of theology.

Finally, I dedicate this work to the trustees, faculty, staff, and students of CTU—my inspiration for all of the twenty-three years I was privileged to serve as president of this vibrant and sacred place.

Introduction

The Gift of Administration

In trying to drive home to his Corinthian community the need for harmony in the midst of diversity, Paul the apostle lists the various gifts that God gives certain people in the community. He begins with what seems a priority list: "first apostles," "second prophets," "third teachers," and then "mighty deeds"—the latter presumably heroic or even miraculous but undefined accomplishments that some perform for the sake of the community. After that Paul lumps other gifts together: "then healing, assistance, administration, and varieties of tongues" (see 1 Cor 12:28). The Greek word Paul uses for "administration" is *kubernetes*, from the root word meaning to "guide" or "steer," like the pilot of a ship.

Curiously, when Paul restates his list in the following verse—reaffirming his message that all those endowed with these various gifts have to work together—he repeats all of the gifts mentioned in the previous verse but leaves out the gift of "administration"! Paul, we should remember, was emphatic about his own role as an apostle, and he testifies that he himself did healings, taught and preached a lot, and was capable of ecstatic utterances, so those gifts loomed large in his own experience. But Paul was never a local administrator, and that particular gift seems to have fallen off of Paul's conscious chart!

Paul's no doubt unintended downplaying of "administration" as a gift of God has been repeated over the centuries and continues to this day. Whole libraries could be filled with contemporary books on the Christian works of teaching, preaching, healing, and prophecy, but there are relatively few biblical or theological studies on administration as a genuine gift or charism for the Church. A few years ago, the Lilly Endowment sponsored two studies of the attitudes of clergy toward administrative and fund-raising activities. They titled the report of these studies, "The Reluctant Steward."[1] They found that while Protestant and Catholic clergy alike prized their work of preaching, counseling, leading worship, and teaching, they considered administrative duties a necessary but unwelcome intrusion on their vocation of ministry.

None of this is a great mystery. The biblical roots of the teaching or preaching ministry, for example, are evident in both the Old and the New Testaments, including the ministry of Jesus himself and the work of the apostles and numerous other characters in the early Church. The work of healing—whether considered from a charismatic perspective or in relationship to the healing arts of the physician and health-care worker—finds a massive foundation in the healing ministry of Jesus and the reverence for the ministry of healing present

1. Daniel Conway, Anita Rook, and Daniel A. Schipp, eds., *The Reluctant Steward: A Report and Commentary on the Stewardship and Development Study* (Indianapolis, IN, and St. Meinrad, IN: Christian Theological Seminary and St. Meinrad Seminary, 1992). A follow-up study appeared ten years later: Daniel Conway, *The Reluctant Steward Revisited: Preparing Pastors for Administrative and Financial Duties; A Report and Commentary on a Study Conducted by Saint Meinrad School of Theology with funding from Lilly Endowment Inc.* (St. Meinrad, IN: St. Meinrad School of Theology, 2002).

throughout the New Testament and on into Church tradition. Obviously the role of the prophet stands out in the Old Testament, and Jesus himself and great leaders of the early Church wore the mantle of the prophet in their fearless proclamation of the Gospel and their challenge to false values.

Administration as a Christian Vocation

But administration as a specific Christian work? Obviously there were leaders and administrators who enabled the early Christian communities to develop and thrive, but their work is not the primary focus of the New Testament and, in a sense, one has to read between the lines of the biblical text to draw out an appreciation of the essential role they played. If today one searches for a deeper understanding of the work of administration from a faith perspective, the terrain of available materials is fairly sparse. Most of the creative reflection on the role of the administrative leader draws on the accumulated wisdom of effective corporate management and utilizes the insights of psychology and other social sciences to address needed skills in areas such as institutional leadership, strategic planning, personnel management, and conflict resolution, as well as how to acquire vital motivational and organizational skills. Popular business "gurus" such as Peter Drucker, Warren Bennis, and Stephen Covey, to cite some noted examples, have published many volumes each and have recorded millions in sales.

In recent years, there has been a growing body of literature that links administration and management with "spirituality."[2]

2. See, for example, Margaret Benefiel, *Soul at Work: Spiritual Leadership in Organizations* (New York: Seabury Press, 2005), and the collection of essays *Religion, Business, and Spirituality*, ed. Oliver F. Williams (Notre Dame, IN: University of Notre Dame Press, 2003).

Many of these works are based on empirical data that gauges the impact of spiritual attitudes and virtues on the effectiveness and satisfaction rates of those who bring their "spirituality" in some fashion into the workplace as opposed to those who do not. By "spirituality," most of these studies mean a set of beliefs and attitudes and a habit of reflection and inner peace that gives a person a certain wisdom and serenity in dealing with the stress of the workplace. Relatively few of these works draw directly on a specific religious tradition such as Christianity, and virtually none connect the specific tasks of administration to the fundamental resources of the Scriptures or Christian theology and Christian faith as such. Employing the values and qualities inherent in one's "spirituality" may increase job satisfaction and help one to cope with the stresses and strains of one's daily work, but there is no case made in these studies to demonstrate how the very tasks of administration are rooted in and are an expression of one's Christian faith or the spirituality that is based on it. On the contrary, administrative work is seen as a challenge to be overcome or a problem to be contained.

Where such rare links between administration and faith are considered, it is often by Evangelical Christians who see administration as a Christian vocation.[3] The body of Roman Catholic authors on this subject is even rarer. One outstanding example is the contribution of Ann M. Garrido in her book *Redeeming Administration: 12 Spiritual Habits for Catholic*

---

3. See, for example, Wayne Grudem, *Business for the Glory of God: The Bible's Teaching on the Moral Goodness of Business* (Wheaton, IL: Crossway Books, 2003); R. J. Stepansky, *Thoughts on Leadership from a Higher Level: Leadership Lessons from the Bible* (Suwanee, GA: Deeper Calling Media, 2015), e-book.

Leaders in Parishes, Schools, Religious Communities and other Institutions, a work that began as a well-received article in *America* magazine and was later expanded into a book.[4] As the subtitle of her work indicates, Garrido reflects on the Christian virtues needed for making the work of administration effective and life giving. She follows her reflections on each of these twelve virtues with an example from the life of a particular saint. In her reflections, she also draws on her own experience in a variety of roles in academic administration at the Aquinas School of Theology in Saint Louis, Missouri. Her list of virtues and her meditations on them will make sense to anyone who has wrestled with the work of administration in various levels of a religious institution: breadth of vision, generativity, trust, *agape* (self-sacrificing love), integrity, humility, courage, a habit of reflection, a sense of humor, willingness to forgive and be forgiven, "embracing death" (i.e., the Christian realization, based on the Paschal Mystery, that some plans and efforts must be transformed by suffering in order to ultimately flourish), and, finally, hope.[5]

If one were to characterize the approach taken in Ann Garrido's study, it might be called an exercise in "virtue ethics" applied to the role of an administrator, that is, identifying the values and practices that promote holiness within the context

---

4. Ann M. Garrido, *Redeeming Administration: 12 Spiritual Habits for Catholic Leaders in Parishes, Schools, Religious Communities, and Other Institutions* (Notre Dame, IN: Ave Maria Press, 2013); also, Ann M. Garrido, "More Than a Desk Job: The Spirituality of Administration," *America* 201, no. 1 (July 6, 2009); Zeni Fox and Regina Bechtle, eds., *Called & Chosen: Toward a Spirituality for Lay Leaders* (Lanham, MD: Rowan and Littlefield, 2005) also take up the issue, but the emphasis in most of the essays included concentrate on ministerial rather than administrative roles.

5. See the further discussion of these "spiritual habits" in chap. 6 below, pp. 137–47.

of a particular role. This is a genuine reflection on Christian spirituality and eminently useful for those who desire to bring the light and wisdom of their Christian and Catholic heritage into the workplace where many Christians will spend a major part of their lives.

The approach taken in *Redeeming Administration* helps clarify the somewhat different—but hopefully complementary—approach I want to take here. Ann Garrido's study—and others similar to it—consider the attitudes and virtues that will enable the Christian to find and exercise virtue in the midst of administrative work. The ultimate goal is to be able to seek and find holiness in this vital and unique form of human activity.

My hope, by contrast, is to consider how the essential elements of the work of administration themselves are rooted in our Christian biblical and theological heritage. While it makes sense to learn the art of administration from the wisdom of corporate leaders and social studies of effective management, what we might call "secular" sources—meant in a positive, not negative sense—it is also important to know that from a Christian perspective, the practices (and virtues) demanded by the work of administration have a solid biblical and theological foundation and as such can be an expression of one's Christian call to discipleship and service. While perhaps not having the explicit and prominent place in the array of Christian ministries that preaching, teaching, and healing may have, nevertheless, administration is also named by Paul as a "gift of God" given to the community to build it into the Body of Christ and one grounded in the very nature of the Christian mission to the world.

For example, the ministry of preaching can learn from the science and art of public speaking and communication, without diminishing the fact that it is an explicit expression of the Christian mission. Those who are Christian teachers can benefit from a study of pedagogy and knowledge of how students at various levels learn, at the same time they can turn to a well-thought-through biblical and systematic theology of Christian teaching that clearly shows this work is an expression of the Gospel. Likewise, those who engage in the healing professions, whether as a physician, nurse, psychologists or research doctor, necessarily depend on the knowledge and skill of the medical profession to responsibly carry out their work, but at the same time, the healing arts are rooted deeply in the very nature of the Christian mission to the world.

I firmly believe that the various expressions of the work of administration, while learning from "secular" experience and knowledge, can also find their grounding and rationale within the very nature of the Christian mission. In short, administration—like preaching, teaching, and healing—is also an expression of the Gospel. To take a quick and perhaps easy example that will be looked at in more depth later on, the work of fund-raising, which many administrators, particularly those at the leadership level, must engage in, can be viewed as a kind of secular activity, with a body of literature that addresses the various techniques and skills needed for this kind of work. But from the perspective of the Christian mission to the world, motivating Christians to share their resources with those in need goes to the heart of the Gospel. Likewise, strategic planning (which will also be considered later), vital for healthy institutions and part of the work of administration, can turn to an enormous "secular" literature on the various methods and philosophies of strategic planning. But at the same time, planning for the future is also a consequence of the Christian view of history, which is rooted in the New Testament itself.

At the heart of Christian ethics is the call for us to live now in view of the future we most earnestly desire to see. Jesus' own inaugural preaching proclaimed that because the kingdom of God was coming we should "change our perspective" (the literal meaning of the Greek word *metanoite* used in the gospel) and believe in the Good News (see Mark 1:14-15). Thus, thinking about the future from the perspective of Christian faith and turning our resources and actions in that direction makes planning a potential act of discipleship.

The Levels of Administration

At the outset, it is important to identify what is meant by administration and who is involved in it. The etymology of the word is revealing. "Administer" comes from Latin, combining the word "serve" (*ministrare*) and the prefix "to" (*ad*), and therefore means to offer aid or service or direction to someone. According to Webster's Dictionary, the word has come to mean in modern English "the process or activity of running a business, organization, etc." The terms "manage" or "manager" can have essentially the same meaning. The verb "manage" comes from the Italian word *maneggiare*, which referred to handling tools or even animals. This word, too, can trace its etymology to the Latin word *manus*, which means "hand." If there is a difference between the concepts of "managing" and "administering," it is that "managing" is often associated with the "handling" or coordinating of personnel within an institution. Sometimes the task of "management" has a somewhat pejorative ring, implying a small-bore type of handling or even manipulating personnel. "Administration," on the other hand, has a broader scope that includes "managing" personnel but incorporates other tasks necessary for the health of an institution.

Thus, an "administrator" is anyone involved in the process of running or managing an institution. Obviously there are different levels of "administration." There are "chief administrators" such as bishops, presidents, deans, finance officers, or directors of development and department heads. And then there are what might be called, especially in the corporate world, "middle management"; these are people such as program directors and key staff. For example, in an academic institution, such key staff include the registrar, the public relations director, the director of maintenance, etc. Then there are the vital roles of the clerical staff such as the receptionists, the security personnel, and so on, whose combined work enables an institution to function. All of these roles and many others like them represent full-time administrative work, i.e., "being involved in the process or activity of running or managing an institution."

There are also persons within an institution—particularly a religious institution such as a parish or school—who do not think of themselves as "administrators" but are, in fact, involved in some aspects of administering an institution. Pastors, for example, are probably reluctant to define themselves as "administrators" but, in fact, they spend a lot of their time involved in the work of administration: worrying about the budget, concerned about leaky roofs and faltering furnaces, and sometimes snarled in difficult personnel issues. In most institutions, faculty, too, would not consider themselves in "administration" but find that their duties include such administrative roles as managing an academic program or heading a department. In the reality of institutional life, the lines between direct administrative work and explicitly pastoral activities can often be blurred. Pastors become immersed in administrative details in order to keep their parish community healthy, and presidents and deans of schools will often have to be "pastors" to some of their faculty and staff in moments of personal crisis. And sometimes, too, the roles seem to merge: having to discipline or even let go of a staff member is one of the administrative responsibilities dreaded by most administrators I know, but there is also the need to carry out this duty in a "pastoral" manner, respecting the dignity and well-being of the person affected.

There is another dimension to the administration of an institution that needs to be identified here as we begin our reflection. I am referring to the notion of "governance." "Governance" may be defined as "the system of rules, practices, and processes by which a company or institution is directed and controlled." Governance implies a certain power or authority to direct an institution in the light of its mission. As such, governance is distinct from "administration" which is more directed to the everyday tasks and procedures and policies that sustain an institution and help it thrive. Within most nonprofit organizations, the category into which most religious institutions fit, "governance" will be the prime responsibility of a Board of Trustees, a bishop, and to some extent the president and chief administrators of an institution who receive delegated authority from their "governing body" and are accountable to that governing body.

In many institutions today, particularly academic ones, there is an interest in "shared governance."[6] Most faculty, for example, do not consider themselves simply as "employees" who

---

6. See the discussion in David Tiede, "Faculty Powers in Shared Governance," *Theological Education* 44 (2009): 29–37; Steven C. Bahls, *Shared Governance in Times of Change: A Practical Guide for Universities and Colleges* (Washington, DC: AGB Press, 2014); also the articles on shared governance found in *In Trust* magazine 26, no. 2 (2015): 19–23.

carry out their responsibilities under the direction of others but as genuine stakeholders in the direction and well-being of the school they serve. They rightly expect to have some say or influence on the overall direction of the school, that is, a share in the school's "governance." This is a reasonable expectation, yet the notion of "shared governance" has a certain imprecision that can lead to misunderstanding and conflict. While faculty, for example, rightly expect that they should be seriously consulted regarding the fundamental direction of the school, that does not necessarily mean that it is a good idea for faculty to have a determining vote on the school's budget or to intrude in contract negotiations. On the other hand, those in administration should not have a heavy hand in designing courses or curriculum. When I first introduced a development program in my school, some faculty members, unused to seeing solicitation letters going out from CTU, wanted to have some say in the content of our appeal letters. Only half in jest, I suggested in that case that I would also want to review each of their syllabi!

"Shared governance" in its healthiest expression means that those who hold ultimate responsibility for the financial and institutional health of the institution exercise that responsibility in a way that recognizes and honors the legitimate concerns that various stakeholders—faculty, staff, and even the wider public—have about the well-being and direction of the school. Such a process of governance calls for a lot of trust and clear communication.

Thus for some major administrators—particularly presidents and other types of chief executive officers—"administration" also involves the responsibility of "governance." Such administrators must not only engage in the day to day tasks of administration but also keep alert to the "bigger picture" and be responsible to the fundamental mission and spirit of an institution. We will consider this further under the heading of "leadership" and its roots in the Gospel.[7]

This book, then, is directed to those who are engaged in governance and administration, whether as full-time administrators and managers or those who define their roles in other ways but are drawn into administrative duties as part of their everyday responsibilities. In the case of academic institutions, I think of the presidents or principals, academic deans and finance officers, development directors and public relations officers, registrars and program directors, directors of maintenance, and the many clerical and other staff that make up the "administration" of a school. In parishes or congregations, I think of the pastor, the business manager or administrator (in parishes where this or a similar role exists), the receptionist and other staff, the school principal, and the building manager—all of whom make up what is often called the "parish staff." And I don't want to exclude those who at least for a portion of their responsibilities are drawn into the work of administration: faculty, teachers, liturgists, etc.

I should make it clear that this is not intended to be a "how to" book, although perhaps some wisdom on how to do the work of administration might slip through! It is more of a "why" book—offering what I hope is a rationale for understanding that the work of administration has as legitimate a claim on the Gospel and the Christian mission as does the more explicit and easily identified work of preaching or teaching or healing. Grasping the "why"—the deeply Christian rationale for the work of administration—can assure us that we are in fact doing the work of God when we serve as

---

7. See chap. 2 below on leadership, pp. 23–42.

an administrator. And that assurance can lead to a deeper serenity about the meaning of our work and even a more effective exercise of it.

When I was first drafted to be president of Catholic Theological Union, I often found myself feeling that I should be somewhere else—that in some strange fashion, I was misplaced. I should be spending more time in biblical research, more time in the classroom, more time with students. I remember sharing this feeling with a trusted colleague who was also a biblical scholar and a president of a major Lutheran seminary. He, too, confessed to sometimes "looking over his shoulder" and wondering if he should be somewhere else. Only after a period of time and, more importantly, after thinking more deeply about the biblical and theological basis for the ministry of administration, did I make peace with my role as president and administrator of an institution and see it more clearly in the light of the Gospel.

Helping others make peace with this Christian task and to draw life from it is the goal of this book.

1

The "Institutional" Church

Is There Another Kind?

One of the fundamental reasons the work of "administration" may be seen as less than wholesome as a Christian calling is because of an aversion to considering the Church itself as an "institution." If you go on the Internet and happen to Google the term "institutional church" or "the church as an institution," you will find item after item stating that the Church is not and should never be an "institution." One author, for example, claims that "the true church is a spiritual organism—a body, not an earthly organization or institution" and appeals to Romans 12:4-5 where Paul states that "we, who are many, are one body in Christ." But in fact the apostle says nothing here for or against the Church as an institution. The same blogger goes on to say, "The bible warned us about the institutional church explaining that it would be a Christian's departure from the faith." Another states: "Words matter. It's potentially dangerous and certainly misleading to refer to the church as an institution. Institutions are by definition an 'it.' The Bible never uses the word 'church' in this fashion."

Yet another observer ratchets things up quite a bit and states unequivocally that "the institutional church is the collected group of Christians who *don't* want a relationship with Jesus Christ on his terms but on their terms. Therefore, they create and serve a false Christ which leads to bondage, a lack of power and a delusional mindset that believes he/she will inherit eternal life when in fact will be damned to hell if there's no repentance." Often enough, the Roman Catholic Church, with its full-blown hierarchical organization and numerous structures, is cited as a prime example of a church that has lost its way by being an institution.

Many of these negative comments about the Church as an "institution" come from Christians who are part of a very charismatic and fundamentalist form of Christianity. Such Christian groups are often described as having a "low ecclesiology"—not "low" in a negative sense but "low" in the sense of being more loosely organized and having minimal structures. But it is not only fundamentalist Christians who take a dim view of the Church as an institution. Some modern biblical scholars and historians tend to speak of early Christianity not as a "church" but as a "movement." Describing the spread of early Christianity as the "Jesus movement" rather than a "church" or "churches" also emphasizes its noninstitutional dimensions, seeing Christianity as an ideology or as a loose collection of diverse groups holding various viewpoints and practices rather than a community with set structures and a visible organization. Prevailing cultural forces may be at work here, too. North Americans, for example, are wary of institutions in general and glory in the freedom and autonomy of the individual. Many Christians today seek spiritual experience but don't want to be part of a religious institution: they are "spiritual but not religious," as the slogan goes.

The Church as an Institution

What is this strong aversion to identifying the Church as an "institution"? We might start by defining what an "institution" is. Webster's Dictionary list several meanings for the term, but the first two on the list are most pertinent:

1. An organization, establishment, foundation, society, or the like, devoted to the promotion of a particular cause or program, especially one of a public, educational, or charitable character: "This college is the best institution of its kind."

2. The building devoted to such a work.

The first meaning probably fits best with what is meant by the "institutional Church"—an organization or human community devoted to a particular "cause" or "program." These are not biblical or traditional Christian terms for the Church, but they do point to a visible human community that is gathered for a particular purpose or, in Christian terms, a particular mission. Sometimes, as in the second definition, we use the term "church" to refer to a building that houses a specific Christian community, but in speaking of the "institutional" Church, we mean something more comprehensive than that— i.e., the entire organization and structure of the Church as a human community.

Of course, the Church is much more than its visible structures. There is what we could call the "charismatic" or "spiritual" dimension of the Church that forms its essence. We are referring here to the faith in Jesus Christ that is the foundation of the Church, to the love of God and neighbor that binds the Church together in community, and to the God-given and Spirit-driven mission of the Church to bring the Gospel message of love and reconciliation to the world. Pope Francis was quoted as saying the "church is not an institution but a relationship of love"—he was no doubt referring to this charismatic or spiritual dimension that gives the Church its ultimate meaning and purpose. Classic Catholic theology referred to three major expressions of the Church: the "Church triumphant," or those Christians who now enjoy God's presence in heaven; the "Church suffering," or those Christians in purgatory awaiting the cleansing of their sins before entering into paradise; and the "Church militant," i.e., the Church on earth still struggling on the path to salvation. All three of these dimensions of the Church have a profound spiritual character—all center on faith in Christ and being animated by God's Spirit of redemptive love.

But, at the same time, the institutional dimension of the "Church militant" is also essential. The Church on earth is composed of bodily human beings who, inspired by God's grace, seek to form a community of faith. And that leads to the requirements of being an "institution." One might ask Pope Francis himself about this as he works on his mandate from the Church to reform its administrative structures! Along with his refreshing emphasis on mercy and forgiveness and the beauty of the Gospel—that is, the Church as "a relationship of love"—Pope Francis has also spent a lot of his time setting up commissions, sorting out the Church's finances, and designing structures and making personnel appointments to give the Church more integrity and make it more efficient. The Church cannot be reduced to its institutional structures, but it also cannot exist without them.

To be a community drawn together and sustained in love and to exist in history with constancy and effectiveness, the Church also needs to be "institutional." Think of this in concrete, practical terms. If the Church is to gather as a community, then it will need physical space in which to do so—whether in someone's home, as was the case with the early Church, or in a structure with enough space and appropriate design set apart for this purpose—as soon developed in Christian history. And if there is such a space, then it might need heat in winter, ventilation in summer, electricity, fuel, maintenance, and money! And if the community grows—as one prays it will and as early Christianity did—then it must have someone to convene the community and gather it and prepare hospitality for its members and lock and unlock the doors and lead or at least facilitate this gathered community in some fashion. And so we have pastors, parish staffs, and various managers and leaders of diverse Church institutions. And if the community is spread out over a certain distance, then this community needs to communicate with its members and instruct them about their faith tradition and preach to them the Gospel message and read to them the Scriptures and teach them how to sing sacred songs—and here come the catechists, the preachers, and the musicians, and here, too, in our modern world, come sound systems and computers, telephones and newsletters, websites, and other forms of social media—and the people with the technical skill to make these things work properly!

And if the Church remains true to what Jesus has commanded his disciples concerning the poor, then the Church is going to have to organize resources to provide food for the poor and other types of social services—and here comes institutions and organizations like Catholic hospitals and clinics, Catholic Charities and Catholic Relief Services and the Saint Vincent DePaul Society and the Knights of Columbus and their counterparts in most Protestant and other Christian denominations—each of them part of the "institutional" dimension of the Church. And if the Church is true to its worldwide mission confided to it by the Risen Christ, then it cannot be confined to a particular place or race or culture, but it must also be regional and international.

Therefore, the Church needs communication and even coordination among the churches (something that was already happening in the earliest Church as attested in the New Testament) and so one needs leadership at a regional and international level—and so we have popes and bishops and Church officials of various sorts and all of the communication structures and lines of authority and coordination and accumulated resources needed to maintain a worldwide community of faith. And, not least, to maintain all this and have things work together properly, the Church needs personnel—many will be volunteers, but many others will need to work full-time as "employees," so they will need just salaries. And, because of the necessary costs of buildings and equipment and hospitality and personnel, there will be a need for collections and fund-raising throughout the Church from its most local expression to its regional and national and international dimensions.

The deepest and most fundamental theological rationale for the Church's necessary institutional character is the incarnation itself. "The Word became flesh and dwelled among us!" This changes everything. Christian faith is not purely "spiritual"; it is also human and physical, rooted in the human body-person and in human history. Jesus of Nazareth, the eternal Son of God, was not a disembodied spirit but a flesh and blood human being—this is ground zero of Christian faith. Catholic tradition has used the lens of the incarnation to understand various aspects of its life. It applies the analogy of the incarnation to the nature of the Scriptures themselves: the Bible is truly God's Word and therefore eminently spiritual, but that Word can only come to us in human terms, incarnate in the various Spirit-illumined writings of the Bible. The biblical authors, we believe, were inspired by the Spirit, but they remained human authors. Therefore, their writings are expressed in and through the language, literary forms, and cultural and scientific limitations of human beings. Unless we were to think of the Scriptures as magical writings that dropped down from the heavens—which we do not—we realize that the Word of God becomes present to us only through human beings. This same incarnational principle can be applied to the sacraments. The visible, physical forms of bread, wine, and oil and the human agency of bride and groom and confessor and anointer make God's transforming grace visible and present and possible for us.

The Human Face of the Church

But, of course, it would be foolish to "idealize" the institutional dimension of the Church. The human face of the Church at times has been and always has the potential to be a cause of scandal and disillusionment for sincere Christians. Certain forms and structures appropriate for the Church's life in one generation can lose their cogency as time and cultures develop and change. The financial resources necessary for the Church to convene and carry out its mission can also become a source of avarice and greed. Church leaders and other personnel necessary for the life of the community can forget their purpose and exist more for themselves, creating a closed clerical or bureaucratic culture. A particular Christian community can close itself off and enjoy the comfort of a close-knit and prosperous religious ghetto while forgetting its mission to the world and ignoring the needs of the poor and vulnerable.

But these failings, which can be inventoried at great length throughout Christian history, do not cancel out the fact that the Church is and must be an "institution" if it is to have a presence in human history and carry out its mission to the world. Many people today, as they have in the past, long for a purely spiritual Church purged of its human dimension, or at least a Church pulsating with full human integrity and Christian devotion—an ideal Church. The popular novelist Anne Rice, who a few years ago converted to Catholicism and later revoked her membership in the Church, stated her reasons for leaving the Church in this way: "For those who care, and I understand if you don't: Today I quit being a Christian. I'm out. I remain committed to Christ as always but not to being 'Christian' or to being part of Christianity. It's simply impossible for me to 'belong' to this quarrelsome, hostile, disputatious, and deservedly infamous group. For ten years, I've tried. I've failed. I'm an outsider. My conscience will allow nothing else." What alienated Anne Rice was not "Christ" but Christians—more precisely, the Church in all its scandalous humanness.

Dietrich Bonhoeffer, the Lutheran pastor and theologian who was martyred by the Nazis at the end of World War II, spoke of this kind of "scandal" in his classic reflection on Christian community, *Life Together*. He and a group of pastors who had taken a prophetic stance against the Nazi regime (a stance which would ultimately cost Bonhoeffer his life) decided to form a clandestine seminary to prepare a new generation of clergy who would not be compromised by collaboration with the Nazi government. Bonhoeffer was asked to write the rule of life for this seminary, and that beautiful and powerful description of Christian life became his book: *Life Together: A Discussion of Christian Fellowship*.[1] In the chapter

1. Dietrich Bonhoeffer, *Life Together: A Discussion of Christian Fellowship* (New York: Harper and Row, 1954).

on "community," Bonhoeffer noted the following: "Innumerable times a whole Christian community has broken down because it had sprung from a wish dream. The serious Christian, set down for the first time in a Christian community, is likely to bring with him a very definite idea of what Christian life together should be and to try to realize it. But God's grace speedily shatters such dreams. . . . He who loves his dream of a community more than the Christian community itself becomes a destroyer of the latter, even though his personal intentions may be ever so honest and earnest and sacrificial."[2] It is the human face of the community—its "institutional" character if you like—that challenges such "wish dreaming," as Bonhoeffer calls it.

The Biblical Foundation for the Institutional Church

A close reading of the New Testament demonstrates that such an "ideal," purely spiritual and suprahuman Church never existed. It is a myth, or what Bonhoeffer would call a "wish dream" to think that the Church of Jesus Christ began as a purely spiritual entity and only degraded into an institution because of the human sinfulness of its members and the compromise of its original ideals. In fact, the Church was an institution from the moment of its birth. Those earnest bloggers who believe it is wrong to view the Church as an institution need to take a deeper look at the Bible, including the portrayal of the frailty and sins of the first few human beings Jesus chose as his community!

Consider Jesus himself and that small community gathered around him as portrayed in the gospels. At first glance, we

---

2. Ibid., 27.

do see that Jesus was a "charismatic" figure, a mobile, itinerant preacher and healer—not an institutional figure such as a leader of a synagogue or a temple priest or official. Yet even within this small and mobile community of followers constituted by Jesus, there are hints of rudimentary institutional life. For example, if John's description of Judas is to be accepted, then this errant disciple was the "treasurer" of this Jesus community, holding the community purse with funds to be used for the group's own needs and to provide alms for the poor (see John 13:29). That there were funds available is suggested by Luke's comment that some prominent women supported Jesus and his disciples out of their own resources (e.g., Joanna, the wife of King Herod's steward Chuza, and "many others"; see Luke 8:3). And we should note that Jesus seems to have "instituted" at least a modest organizational structure among his community of disciples, with Peter designated as the leader and spokesperson (Matt 16:17-19, a role echoed in all four of the gospels). When faced with a hungry crowd who had no provisions on hand and were in an isolated spot, Jesus instructs his disciples to organize things and exercise some crowd control! (Mark 6:39-40, where Jesus tells his disciples to organize the crowd in groups of "hundreds and fifties.")

But much more important than these few hints of some rudimentary institutional life among the band of Jesus' disciples is the glaring fact that Jesus himself was a full participant in a longstanding religious institution, namely, Judaism. Jesus of Nazareth, after all, did not come to found a new religious institution or church; in a very real sense, the "church" or the *ekklesia*—the "assembly" of God from which the term "church" ultimately derives—was already there in the religion of which Jesus was a part, the covenant community of Israel instituted by God at Sinai. It would be more accurate to say that the earthly Jesus' more immediate mission was to reform and reinvigorate his religious community, his beloved Judaism, rather than to start something completely different. Only later, under the inspiration of the Risen Christ and the unfolding events of the post-Easter community and its mission, would—over time—the distinctive existence of the Christian Church vis à vis Judaism become apparent.

But during his lifetime, it is clear that Jesus participated readily in the "institutional" life of the Jewish community. The signs are everywhere in the gospels. As several stories of Jesus' healing and teaching in all four gospels demonstrate, Jesus frequented the synagogues of his region. As Luke begins his description of the ministry of Jesus, he notes: "He came to Nazareth, where he had grown up, and went according to his custom into the synagogue on the Sabbath day" (Luke 4:16). Mark's Gospel, too, notes that Jesus' first exorcism—at the very beginning of his ministry—took place in the synagogue of Capernaum (Mark 1:21-28). Matthew summarizes Jesus' ministry thus: "He went around all of Galilee, teaching in their synagogues, proclaiming the gospel of the kingdom, and curing every disease and illness among the people" (Matt 4:23; a summary statement repeated in 9:35). In describing Jesus' discourse on the Bread of Life, John's Gospel notes, "These things he said while teaching in the synagogue of Capernaum" (John 6:59).

The synagogue we now know from the past several decades of archaeological exploration in the Holy Land was a vital Jewish institution that existed alongside the Jerusalem temple and was the source of local Jewish communities' prayer life, education, and social interaction. Synagogues were administered by "managers" and attendants—presumably compensated by the synagogue community for their services. Rabbis, on the other hand, served as the source of religious teaching and preaching for the synagogue congregations. In Luke's account of the healing of the woman "bent double" (Luke

13:10-17), Jesus has an encounter with an anxious synagogue "manager" (literally in Greek, the *archisynagogos* or "leader" of the synagogue) who, despite witnessing the cure of the woman (whom Jesus calls a "daughter of Abraham"), worries about the schedule: "There are six days when work should be done. Come on those days to be cured, not on the Sabbath." How many administrators over the centuries have also worried about the schedule! Luke also notes that in Nazareth a synagogue "attendant" (in Greek, the *huperetos*, that is, an "attendant" or "servant") provides Jesus with the scroll from which this visiting preacher will read and preach (Luke 4:17, 20). Both of these passages suggest a level of institutional organization in the synagogue life of the time.

We also know that Jesus frequented the Jerusalem temple—clearly a major sacred institution for Judaism and one that would remain sacred for early Christianity until the tragic destruction of this massive shrine in AD 70, as we learn from the early chapters of Acts (see Acts 2:42-47). In Luke, Jesus' family takes the infant Jesus to the temple for a blessing as prescribed by the Mosaic Law (Luke 2:22-24). Later, when Jesus and his family have come on pilgrimage to Jerusalem for the bar mitzvah of Jesus, he is separated from them because he loves being in the temple and being in conversation with some of the teachers and priests associated with the temple (Luke 2:41-50). All three Synoptic Gospels portray Jesus' final visit to the temple as the climax of his earthly mission (see Mark 11; Matt 21; Luke 19). His prophetic action of purifying the temple triggers deadly opposition to Jesus and will lead ultimately to his death. John's Gospel, on the other hand, recounts several visits of Jesus to the temple and his involvement in the liturgies associated with the temple.[3]

---

3. See John 2:13-25; 5:1; 7:10, 37; 10:22; 12:12; 13:1-2.

Later Christian literature, especially after the destruction of the temple by the Romans in AD 70, would describe the body of the Risen Jesus as the "temple" where God dwelled (as in the case of John's Gospel, see John 2:19-22) or see the Christian community itself as the "temple"—now a spiritual temple not made by hands and, like the Jerusalem temple before it, as the locus of God's presence.[4]

The gospels are clear that Jesus reverenced the temple— this massive institution—otherwise he would not have been distraught at the abuses that detracted from its sacredness. Because the Jerusalem temple had been built by Herod the Great whose own religious integrity was very suspect, some devout Jews foresaw that in the messianic age to come God would destroy the building constructed under Herod and replace it with a new and purified temple.[5] But in any case, Jesus, like his fellow Jews, had great reverence for this "house of God" and went there to offer sacrifice, to pray, and to learn.

There is no question that the temple was an "institution" by any definition. For it to function, it needed elaborate systems: a water system for the constant animal sacrifices that took place there; a host of priests and attendants to ensure the smooth functioning of the temple liturgies and for crowd control; workers who cleaned and maintained the temple; money changers to convert Roman coins (with the head of the emperor inscribed on it) into specially minted coins suitable for a temple donation; shops to take care of those seeking to purchase doves and grains for sacrifice and to attend to the

---

4. See, for example, 1 Cor 3:16-17; 6:19; 2 Cor 6:16; Eph 2:21-22; 1 Pet 2:4-5.

5. See Donald Juel, *Messiah and Temple*, SBL Dissertation Series (Missoula, MT: Scholars Press, 1977); Nicholas Perrin, *Jesus the Temple* (Grand Rapids, MI: Baker Academic, 2010).

needs of the thousands of pilgrims who came to the temple each year; *mikvot* or ritual baths needed so that the devout pilgrims who came could properly purify themselves before entering the sacred precincts of the temple; and so on.

And Jesus, too, participated—as virtually all male Jews did—in the financial upkeep of the temple and its priest-hood. That ancient Judaism had an elaborate system of tithing in order to provide funds for the personnel and activities of the temple is well known. An intriguing story in Matthew's Gospel portrays Jesus as instructing Peter to extract a coin from the mouth of a fish so that it could cover the half-shekel temple tax that each of them—and all male Jews—were expected to pay (Matt 17:24-27). And Jesus praises the poor widow who gives so generously to the upkeep of the temple (Mark 12:41-44).

Thus to claim that Jesus was fundamentally opposed to his community becoming an "institution" runs contrary to the actual evidence of the gospels. Jesus himself was a full and devout participant in the institutional life of his own Jewish religion. He strongly critiqued the false values and hypocrisy of many of the religious leaders and their practices, but that did not lead Jesus to avoid participating in synagogue life or to refuse to enter the temple. It also meant that Jesus, like his fellow Jews, depended on the people and structures and systems that enabled the temple and the synagogue to function. And, like his fellow Jews, Jesus contributed financially to the upkeep of this "institution."

The Apostolic Church as Institution

The biblical case for the Church as an institution is even more evident in looking closely at the life of the early Church as depicted in the other writings of the New Testament. The apostolic Church and the post–New Testament Church would fight hard to maintain their fundamental belief in the humanity of Jesus. The Risen Christ present in the community through the power of the Spirit was also the earthly Jesus who had been crucified and who still bore those wounds as a sign of his love. In the remarkable and haunting resurrection appearance stories in the Gospels of Luke and John the Risen Christ appears to his disciples with the marks of the nails of crucifixion visible on his risen and transformed body (see Luke 24:39-40; John 20:20). In Matthew's Gospel, the Risen Christ promises to remain with his fragile and hesitant community until the end of time (Matt 28:16-20), fulfilling his name as "Emmanuel—God-With-Us (see Matt 1:23). Paul, of course, would forge a designation for the Church that drew directly on the mystery of the incarnation. The Church was the "Body of Christ" and its many and diverse members were formed by the very human participants in the Church that Paul names (see 1 Cor 12:12-31; Rom 12:3-8; also picked up in Eph 4:1-16; and Col 2:9-10).

The Church of the New Testament founded in the wake of the resurrection of Christ was from the start a very human church, no less so than the community of very human and very frail human beings whom Jesus had chosen as his first disciples. The gospels do not flinch from describing the confusion, failings, and outright sins of Jesus' disciples. One will betray him, the leader denies he even knows Jesus, and all of the disciples seem to abandon Jesus at his time of greatest need. The mission of the Church was to bring the presence and message of Jesus to the world, but it would do so through the human agency of the disciples and the structures—institutions—they built.

Those institutional structures and functions are found on almost every page of the New Testament. Because we learn about these structures through comments and asides in letters and other texts, we do not have the benefit of a full description of the Church's organization in the New Testament period. But we have plenty of evidence that the Church became organized from the outset—probably adapting structures they were used to in Judaism since the majority of the first generation of followers of Jesus was Jewish. We hear about "elders" (*presbyters*) who are not just older and hopefully wiser members of the community but also have an official role (1 Tim 5:17-22). We hear of "overseers" or "bishops" (the Greek term *episcopoi* is used for both; see 1 Tim 3:1-7), leaders whose original function seemed to be primarily managing the financial resources of the communities but later expanded to other related supervisory duties.[6] There are "widows" who also seem to have official duties (1 Tim 5:3-16). Luke tells us that the Jerusalem community selected "deacons" to take care of the distribution of goods to those in need so that others could devote themselves to the preaching ministry (Acts 6:1-7; also mentioned in 1 Tim 2:8-13). Paul has his trusted companions such as Timothy, Titus Sosthenes, Silas, and others who traveled with him and frequently carry his pastoral letters and other messages to the various communities the apostle had visited. The Jerusalem Church sent the highly respected and trustworthy Barnabas to investigate the situation in Antioch where some Jewish Christians had started baptizing Gentiles. Later the Church in Antioch would commission Paul and Barnabas to begin a mission to the rest of Asia Minor.

---

6. See Alistair C. Stewart, *The Original Bishops: Office and Order in the First Christian Communities* (Grand Rapids, MI: Eerdmans, 2014).

The early Church also had a fairly sophisticated level of organization that extended beyond a local community. Acts informs us that the community in Antioch wanted to send some financial support to the Christians in Judea who were suffering from a famine. After organizing a collection they sent the always trusted Barnabas, along with Paul, to deliver the contribution to the elders of Jerusalem (Acts 11:29-30). Peter, James, Paul, Barnabas, and other apostolic leaders arrange to gather in Jerusalem to tackle the issue of the mission to the Gentiles and its requirements (Acts 15)—the timing and communication and arrangements for such a meeting demand a fairly advanced level of organization. There is also evidence of other such formal meetings taking place in the early Church (e.g., Acts 20:17-28 where Paul arranges a meeting with the elders of Ephesus at Miletus as he is on his way by ship to Jerusalem).

These and other early Christian leaders were human beings and had to eat and pay their expenses—presumably with financial support supplied by their sponsoring Christian communities. Paul, in fact, emphasizes that leaders and missionaries like himself had a right to financial support from the community, even though he generally chose to support himself with his tent-making work (see 1 Cor 9:1-18). In his letter to the Philippians—a community Paul obviously favored—the apostle thanks the community for its monetary support of his mission (see Phil 4:15-18).[7] And, as we will discuss in more detail later, Paul would initiate a major fund-raising campaign among the Gentile churches for the sake of the

---

7. On this, see Julien M. Ogereau, "Paul's κοινωνία with the Philippians: Societas as a Missionary Funding Strategy," *New Testament Studies* 60 (2014): 360–78; and D. E. Briones, *Paul's Financial Policy* (New York: T & T Clark, 2013).

Church in Jerusalem.[8] The Acts of the Apostles tells us that the Jerusalem Christians "shared all things in common" and pooled their resources. The fateful story of Ananias and Sapphira who are struck dead because they deceived the apostles about their finances indicates how serious this "institutional" aspect of the early Church was taken![9]

We also know that the early Church selected places in which to meet. Paul refers to various groups of Christians at Corinth who gather in specific homes, probably villas capable of holding a fairly sizeable group. Paul writes to his friend Philemon and "to the church that gathers in your house" (Phlm 2). Clearly in these homes where the community gathered on a regular basis, the "hosts" not only provided space and hospitality but also exercised a certain leadership—enough to have some of the Christians identify with them (see 1 Cor 1:10-17). As time went on and the communities grew, these original house churches would give way to larger buildings specifically designated for Christian gatherings and worship.

There was also considerable communication among the various local Christian communities—not just casual friendly relations but apostolic communications from sets of Christian leaders to their fellow Christians. Obviously this is the case with Paul who sends letters to his various churches, a practice continuing beyond the lifetime of Paul and into the life of the post-New Testament apostolic Church as indicated in the *Didache* and the Letters of Clement, Ignatius, and Polycarp that extend into the second century. The author of the First Letter of Peter, for example, foresees his message being delivered to a series of Christian communities in north and central Asia Minor (i.e., in the regions of "Pontus, Galatia,

8. See below, pp. 114–15, 125–30.
9. See Acts 5:1-11.

Cappadocia, Asia, and Bithynia"—all regions in present-day Turkey). Although we know less about the specific details of how they were circulated, the gospels, too, must have quickly spread throughout the Christian world of the first century. Both Matthew and Luke were acquainted with the Gospel of Mark and there is also some level of contact or at least influence between the Synoptic Gospels and the Gospel of John.

In any case, by the end of the first century the gospels and the Pauline letters and most of the other New Testament writings were known and accepted as sacred writings. This implies a remarkable network of organization and communication on the part of the early Church. It also requires financial organization, with support needed to compose and preserve copies of scrolls and to provide for the livelihood of at least some Christians who were entrusted with circulating—and in some instances interpreting—such texts. Much of their support would come from the hospitality of the communities who received these messengers, but this local hospitality would not be available everywhere and no doubt some direct financial support must have been supplied to the early Christian missionaries and teachers who circulated on land and sea throughout the Mediterranean world.[10]

A Fully Human Church

As is the case today, these institutional structures and the personnel who administered them—this necessary human

---

10. The *Didache*, a Christian text that may date to the end of the first century, advises the communities to offer hospitality to itinerant prophets and teachers but to be wary of those who are frauds or take advantage of such hospitality. On this see Thomas O'Loughlin, *The Didache: A Window on the Earliest Christians* (Grand Rapids, MI: Baker Academic, 2010), esp. pp. 105–28.

face of the Church—would be the cause of stress, failure, and scandal from the very beginning of the Church's existence. Very often finances and other resources became a source of conflict. This was the case with the Jerusalem Church, as is noted in the Acts of the Apostles (6:1-7); apparently the Greek-speaking Jewish Christians were complaining about the Hebrew-speaking Jewish Christians because the widows of the Greek speakers were being neglected in the daily distribution of food. The leadership had to step in and appoint assistants who would take care of the problem. As noted above, John's Gospel accuses Judas of pilfering from the common purse he had been entrusted with (see John 12:4-6). The sharp words of the Johannine letters about the "deceivers" seem to warn the community addressed to be careful about offering hospitality and support to these interlopers (see 2 John 8-10). Paul makes a sharp defense of his and Barnabas's rights to receive support from the Corinthian community—apparently in response to criticism he had received from some members of the community (see 1 Cor 9:1-18).

There were also disputes and clashes in the early Church, just as there have been through the centuries. Paul reports confronting Peter "to his face" when the leader of the apostles had withdrawn from table fellowship with Gentiles in Antioch, apparently because Peter had been criticized by representatives of James and the Jerusalem Church (Gal 2:11-14). Paul and Barnabas, the first missionary team in the early Church, decide to break up when Paul opposes having John Mark accompany them because he had apparently abandoned them at Pamphylia during their first missionary journey (Acts 15:36-41). Paul wrestles with his Corinthian Christians on a number of disputed points, including the division of the community into factions (1 Cor 1:10-11). Paul also urges Euodia and Syntyche, apparently two prominent women in the community of Philippi, to reconcile with each other and asks others in the community to be mediators (Phil 4:2-3). The letters of John, particularly the second and third letters, reveal a community engulfed in bitter controversies concerning rival factions and false teachers. James confronts his community about showing partiality during their assembly to the rich while embarrassing the poor (Jas 2:1-4). The author of 2 Peter warns that there are some statements in Paul's letters "hard to understand" which can lead the ignorant and unstable astray (2 Pet 3:14-16). And strong complaints about false teachers leading the community astray are found throughout the New Testament, especially in the Pastoral Epistles (e.g., 2 Tim 2:16-18, which names Hymenaeus and Philetus as false teachers whose corrupt influence "will spread like gangrene"!). As we will point out later, there is a substantial amount of exhortation in the New Testament letters about avoiding recriminating and provocative speech and the need for community members to address each other with respect and care—a sure sign that disputes were not uncommon in the early Church![11] No wonder that in Jesus' discourse on life in the community of disciples, the Gospel of Matthew provides a procedure for handling conflict as well as an urgent call for limitless forgiveness (see Matt 18:15-20).

Conclusion

There is no doubt that from the very outset the Church of Jesus Christ, along with its vibrant faith and dynamic missionary spirit, was also a very human Church—human in its need to organize and structure its life together in order

---

11. See below, pp. 82–93.

to exist within history and human in that it was prone to problems and failures. As we have noted in the examples cited in this chapter, there are clear signs of the Church's essential "institutional" nature from the first moment of its existence, including the experience of Jesus himself and his small community of disciples embedded within their Jewish context. Obviously the often rudimentary structures of the early Church would develop and change as the Church moved out further into the Mediterranean world and grew in size and complexity. Obviously, too, a community of believers that existed as a small and fragile minority within an often hostile Roman world would undergo significant change when in the post-Constantinian period of the fourth century and beyond, it would receive imperial endorsement. But no matter what these historical developments entailed, it is a myth to describe the change as that of an original, purely spiritual, charismatic, and noninstitutional Church degrading into an institutional Church essentially alien in form and spirit from the Church Jesus intended.

A Church built on faith in the incarnate Jesus and one extending its life out into history would by necessity be an institutional Church, with strengths and weaknesses not unlike those of the institutional Church today. If I have learned anything from spending many years in administration, it is that institutions have a life of their own! An institution is formed of a network of people and structures that cannot be ignored. If the Church has an institutional dimension, then it also needs administrators of various sorts to enable the Church to continue its journey through history. It is to the various facets of administration within the context of a community of faith and their foundation in the Gospel that we now turn.

2

Institutional Leadership

"Come, Follow Me"

One of the key roles in the administration of any institution, including a religious one, is leadership. There is a vast library of works on leadership, most of it focused on the experience of leadership in the corporate world. A recent exploration of Amazon.com reveals a listing of the "One hundred best books on leadership," beginning with Stephen Covey's *The 7 Habits of Highly Effective People: Powerful Lessons in Personal Change* and concluding with Patrick Lincioni's *The Five Dysfunctions of a Team: A Leadership Fable*. While there is much practical wisdom to be learned from this body of literature, our goal here is not to try to summarize these materials or to offer yet another model for effective institutional leadership but to ask how certain essential aspects of institutional leadership can be seen as a fundamental expression of Christian faith and ministry.

Defining Leadership

We can begin by asking: what is "leadership"? The term can be defined in innumerable ways; one of the clearest and most succinct definitions I have come across is this: leadership "is the ability to influence others toward a common mission."[1] Through personal example and inspiration, through organizational skill and effective communication, and with persevering effort, the leader can move others to work together for a common purpose.

There are obviously different levels and types of leadership. Some leadership is exercised by those who hold formal positions of authority: pastors, bishops, presidents, directors, principals, etc. Other examples of leadership are more "charismatic" or "informal" in nature. For example, a natural leader can emerge from a gathering or a town meeting that has very little formal structure until someone with leadership ability stands up and gives it direction and force. The charismatic leader has the gift of speaking for the group and expressing in a forceful and inspiring way the deep yearnings of the people involved. In the midst of a crisis or emergency, charismatic and heroic leaders can suddenly emerge to lead people to safety or quell panic on the part of a crowd.

There is also a distinction between "formal" and "informal" leadership. Those who hold designated positions of authority in an organization automatically exercise a kind of formal leadership. But the persons who hold such positions are not necessarily skilled or effective "leaders"—sometimes they do not have the personal capacity "to influence others toward a common mission." On the other hand, there can be people in an organization or movement who, while not having the formal authority of an official position, yet become the real "leaders" to whom people turn for guidance and inspiration.

---

1. G. Douglass Lewis and Lovett H. Weems Jr., eds., *A Handbook for Seminary Presidents* (Grand Rapids, MI: Eerdmans, 2006), 10.

It is also self-evident that leadership within any movement or organization will be exercised at various levels. Some may be the designated head of an organization; others may be senior administrators who share with the top leadership responsibility for the good of the organization as a whole. Still others exercise leadership over various sectors of an organization or movement; they are not responsible for the overall functioning of the organization, but their sector is an important part of the operation, and they have to work in harmony with the mission and policies of the organization in order to be effective leaders.

Our focus here is on "institutional leadership," that is, leadership exercised, both formally and informally, and at various levels, within a religious institution: a diocese, a parish, a school, a diocesan agency, a religious community, a religiously sponsored hospital or clinic, a religious community or organization. So we might adapt the definition of leadership noted above: "Institutional leadership is the ability to influence others toward the mission of a specific institution." This form of leadership applies to senior administrators (the pastor, the bishop, the president, the provincial, the principal, the director, etc.) as well as to those coworkers who exercise administration at various other levels within an institution.

Experience and common sense identify certain key responsibilities for such institutional leadership:

1. The leaders of an institution have to keep focused on its mission and be faithful to it. This applies in a particular way to senior administrators, but it is also a responsibility of all those who work for a particular institution. Being faithful to an institution's mission, as we will note below, also implies the ongoing adaptive work needed to

keep the institution's mission fresh and responsive to the evolving context in which the institution lives.[2]

2. The leaders of an institution also have the responsibility to coordinate and guide the efforts of the various components that make up the institution. This means keeping in mind the well-being and needs of the institution as a whole and striving to keep the various components in a healthy balance and working harmony.

3. It is also the responsibility of institutional leaders—particular senior administrators—to secure the personal, financial, and structural resources (e.g., clear lines of authority and communication, proper equipment, etc.) necessary for the effective carrying out of the institution's mission. The blunt slogan—"no margin, no mission"—is true! Without the resources truly needed to operate, even the most noble and worthy institutions fail. Accordingly, it is not enough to secure needed resources; the administration of an institution also is responsible that its resources are used wisely—good stewardship is an essential quality of effective administrative leadership. One of the driving goals of the administration of an institution is to create the proper environment in which the work of the institution can thrive.

4. In some cases, it falls to the leadership of an institution to also ensure good relationships with the wider world it serves. For example, the pastor should have good relations with local civil officials and with other neighboring religious leaders, not to mention the diocese of which

2. See below, pp. 52–66.

the parish is a part; the president of a school of theology has to help donors, church officials, and the wider public understand the mission of theological education and support it. One analyst has named this function "fending off enemies"! This, too, can be a responsibility of an institutional leader, i.e., keeping alert to what outside forces might have a destructive effect on an institution's mission (e.g., the threat of an economic downturn, bad publicity, the opposition of religious or civil leaders, serious duplication and competition from peer institutions, etc.). Thus the leader must also represent the institution to its vital outside constituencies and be informed enough about the surrounding world to alert his or her colleagues to key issues and factors that could either help their institution thrive or threaten its future.

In this chapter we will give special attention to the first two responsibilities of institutional leadership and take up the others in subsequent chapters.

The Biblical Roots of Leadership

Because the Bible is rooted in the history of a people as it unfolded over centuries, leaders of various sorts appear on every page. We think of the great patriarchs cited in the books of Genesis, Exodus, and Deuteronomy: Abraham who, when beckoned by God, leads his clan and his cattle out of Ur of the Chaldeans and into the land of Canaan; Joseph, abandoned for dead by his brothers, is miraculously delivered and rises to become the chief advisor and administrator for the Pharaoh of Egypt; Moses and Aaron, given the arduous and often thankless task of leading the Israelites across the Sinai desert in search of the Promised Land. The parade of great leaders continues throughout the biblical saga: Joshua organizing and leading Israel's conquest of the land; kings such as the great David and his son Solomon who bring the people of Israel to their most powerful moments in history; the moral leadership of the prophets such as Amos, Isaiah, and Jeremiah who became the public conscience of Israel; Ezra and Nehemiah who organize the rebuilding of Jerusalem and Judea after the devastation of the Babylonian exile.

Jesus the Leader

This inventory of leadership continues in the New Testament as well, definitively and most fundamentally with Jesus himself. Jesus, of course, is the leader par excellence, the inspiration for everything that would emerge in the life of the early Church. If we were to try to put Jesus into a leadership category, he would not be an "institutional" or "formal" leader but a definitive "charismatic" leader. Jesus was a layperson, neither priest nor ruler. But Jesus taught in such a way that the crowds were "astonished" at his teaching (Matt 7:28-29), because he spoke with "authority and not as the scribes" (Mark 1:23). Jesus, whose teaching drew on the deepest and most authentic traditions of his Jewish heritage and thereby gave those who heard him a sense of their own God-given dignity. Jesus, whose vivid words and images enflamed human hearts and moved the spirits of those drawn to him while leaving his toxic opponents speechless. Jesus, whose power to heal bound up the physical and psychological wounds of his people—people not only afflicted with illness but also wounded by economic exploitation and the violence inflicted by crude and oppressive rulers. Jesus, who fearlessly confronted the injustice that burdened the poor, fed the hungry crowds, and boldly challenged the hypocrisy of the religious and civil leaders of his day. Jesus, who evoked a blessed future in which those who mourned, those who were trampled down by others, those who were disinherited and suffered persecution, would be vindicated by God and shed no more tears. Jesus, who had not come to be served but who would give his life in service to others, even to the point of crucifixion engineered by hostile religious authorities and the brutality of Roman imperial power. Jesus, who when all was said and done, had revealed an exercise of messianic authority that confounded the oppressive and exploitive power that most people had experienced from their leaders.

The immediate mission of Jesus of Nazareth was to restore his beloved Israel, the people of God, to draw together in peace and justice those who had been scattered by violence and conflict and injustice. Thus we find Jesus' characteristic images of seeking the lost sheep, searching for the lost coin, waiting intensely for the return of the lost son, and opening place at the banquet table for those in the highways and byways.

It was this Jesus—this "leader"—who would invite startled fishermen, unsuspecting toll collectors, and other men and women to "come, follow me." All exercise of Christian leadership, in whatever form it would take from the beginning of the Church until today, must find its inspiration and example in the qualities of Jesus' own leadership. The disciple can only strive to be like the Master.

Peter, Paul, and Barnabas

Such was the case with that towering figure of the New Testament, Paul the apostle. Paul, too, falls into the category of the charismatic rather than that of the "administrative" leader. Although Paul founded several Christian communities in Asia Minor and Macedonia and was an inspiration for many previously founded communities (e.g., Corinth, Rome, Ephesus), he did not exercise administrative leadership over any of them. Paul apparently stayed for extended periods of several months in a few places such as Antioch, Corinth, Ephesus, and later in Rome, but his role was more that of a charismatic preacher, teacher, and animator rather than the one who organized and supervised the life and structures of these communities. Some have wryly observed that Paul had a turbulent relationship with the one community where he may have spent the longest time—namely, Corinth!

Paul himself seems to be aware that his best role was that of an itinerant preacher spreading the Gospel where no one else had already evangelized: "Thus I aspire to proclaim the gospel not where Christ has already been named, so that I do not build on another's foundation" (Rom 15:20). Paul was determined, courageous, tireless, and passionate about his love for Christ. His letters probed deeply into the mystery of Christ and presented bold challenges and loving inspiration for the communities to which they were sent. He would prove an unyielding champion of the Gentile mission, convinced that God was reaching out to them just as much as God had embraced Paul's beloved Jewish brothers and sisters. Paul was the definition of a charismatic leader.

As we will note later, Paul was also acutely conscious not only of the bond that should exist within a local Christian community, whether in Philippi or Corinth, but also the bond that held together the entire network of local churches with the mother church in Jerusalem. Thus Paul, like his Master, exercised his charismatic leadership for the common good of the entire Christian community, for the whole Body of Christ. Paul would attempt one of the most complicated organizational efforts of his life—the collection from all of the Gentile churches on behalf of the mother church in Jerusalem—as a practical expression to the bond of love and generosity and gratitude that should characterize the whole Body of Christ. In this way, surely Paul was a preeminent leader of the early community, even though it appears that when this accumulated gift was brought to Jerusalem the local community there was wary of what Paul intended.[3]

The other prominent leadership figure in the New Testament is Peter, and here we move closer to the kind of institutional leadership we have been concentrating on. The multiple references to Peter in the gospels as the spokesperson for that fragile community of disciples suggests that already during the lifetime of Jesus, this fisherman turned disciple was given some form of particular responsibility or leadership by Jesus. In the famous scene in Matthew's Gospel (16:16-19), Jesus designates Peter as the "rock" on which he would build his Church and gives to Peter "the keys of the kingdom of heaven"—words that echo those of Isaiah 22:22 where God designates Hilkiah to be the "prime minister" of the House of David. Peter is consistently identified as the first of the disciples called by Jesus. And Peter is given privileged access to key moments of Jesus' life: his transfiguration on the mountaintop, his anguished prayer in Gethsemane, and his trial before the High Priest. Peter speaks on behalf of the other disciples: answering Jesus' question about his identity, asking about what reward the disciples might expect for following him, relaying to Jesus the question of the religious leaders

3. See below, pp. 125–30.

about paying the temple tax, asking the "Beloved Disciple" in John's Gospel about the identity of Jesus' betrayer. And with the discovery of the empty tomb on Easter Sunday, it is Peter who is given deference by the Beloved Disciple to be the first to inspect the place where the body of the Crucified Jesus had laid. Even Paul, who had his tensions with Peter, notes that this apostle was the first to encounter the Risen Christ (1 Cor 15:5).

Peter's leadership role continues in the early Church and here his role takes on a more formal nature. The Acts of the Apostles notes that Peter fearlessly speaks to the crowds and confronts the Jerusalem authorities on several occasions, even at the risk of imprisonment. Along with John, Peter is able to heal the man who is paralyzed at the temple gate and to do so in the name of Jesus. But we also see indications of Peter's organizational authority as someone who holds the community together as it must navigate several challenges early in its evolving mission. It is Peter who convenes the community to select Judas's successor. At the event of Pentecost, faced with a crowd who has come from all points of the Mediterranean world, it is Peter, on behalf of the community, who interprets for them what is happening. Peter is the one who has to deal with the frightening and tragic case of Ananias and Sapphira who are dishonest with the community about their resources. And Peter is the one who refuses the bribe offered by Simon, the Samaritan magician who wanted to buy his way into discipleship.

One of the most important steps taken by Peter as leader of the community is related in the dramatic and extensive account Luke gives of the conversion of the Roman centurion Cornelius at Caesarea Maritima, the official site of Roman imperial authority in Judea (see Acts 10:1–11:18). Napping on a rooftop while waiting for his lunch in the port city of Joppa, Peter has a dream in which God invites him to eat non-kosher foods. Peter protests: "Certainly not, sir. For never have I eaten anything profane and unclean" (Acts 10:14). But God has another perspective: "What God has made clean, you are not to call profane." And then Peter is sent on his way up the coast to Caesarea where he meets Cornelius and his household. Before Peter even can finish his theological soliloquy, God's Spirit falls upon this Roman officer and his family and thus the first Gentile converts enter the Christian community! It is left to Peter, the leader of the community, to discern what is happening: "In truth I see that God shows no partiality. Rather, in every nation whoever fears him and acts uprightly is acceptable to him" (10:34-35).

Note that it is not sufficient for Peter to be the means by which the horizon of the Jewish-Christian community would now expand to include the Gentiles, but, like many leaders since, Peter had to help the rest of the community understand and accept this momentous turn of events. He returns to Jerusalem and explains everything that had happened. At last the Christian leaders in Jerusalem see the light: When they heard this, they stopped objecting and glorified God, saying, 'God has then granted life-giving repentance to the Gentiles too' (11:18).

Luke dwells on this incident because it represents one of the greatest challenges the early Church faced—should their mission extend beyond the boundary of Judaism to include the Gentiles and, if so, under what conditions. It seems clear that Peter, designated as the "rock" of Jesus' community, actually played a significant mediating role in the process of accepting the Gentile mission—and thus exercised true administrative leadership. The power of "binding and loosing" given to

Peter by Jesus echoes Jewish terminology about determining membership within the community. Peter will be portrayed as a key figure at the Council of Jerusalem described in Acts 15 that dwelt precisely with this problem. When the "apostles and elders" conclude their debate about this complex issue, Peter is the one who stands up and gives the decisive perspective: "My brothers, you are well aware that from early days God made his choice among you that through my mouth the Gentiles would hear the word of the gospel and believe. And God, who knows the heart, bore witness by granting them the Holy Spirit just as he did us" (15:6-8).

Peter seems to have continued this key mediating role as the early Church navigated its way through this cultural and theological boundary issue. Although we hear of the incident at Antioch through the vantage point of Paul, one can understand Peter's difficult position. In Antioch, where a number of Gentiles had been received in the community, Peter at first had joined these Gentile converts at meals, where presumably non-kosher food was served (see Gal 2:11-14). But when messengers from James, the leader of the strict Jewish-Christian faction in Jerusalem, appeared on the scene and protested this practice, Peter drew back and no longer shared these type of meals. Paul takes great offense at this, considers it "hypocrisy" and publicly confronts both Barnabas and Peter. Peter, like later generations of administrators trying to make peace in the institutional family, was labeled a "hypocrite" and accused of compromising his ideals. Yet, from the viewpoint of a key administrative leader, Peter was also trying to keep a badly divided Christian community together—attempting to maintain ties with the Gentile Christians while also respecting the sensitivities of the stricter Jewish-Christian and founding community of Jerusalem. Even though Paul in this instance leaves no room for compromise, later, when he himself was faced with practical questions from the Corinthians about the issue of eating meat that had been offered to idols, he counsels his Christians there not to offend the conscience of those who are sensitive about this issue![4] Sometimes, those who exercise administrative leadership cannot afford a "pure" viewpoint but, for the sake of the common good, have to balance differing stances among members of the community as a whole.

Peter would continue to be a leader of the early Church, helping it navigate its future mission in both the Gentile and Jewish worlds. Letters in the name of Peter would be sent from Rome to a series of local churches in northern Asia Minor and there is a strong historical probability that Peter spent time in Rome where he would also die a martyr's death.[5] That destiny seems to be hinted at in the concluding chapter of John's Gospel. Peter, who had publicly denied his Master at the moment of his trial in Jerusalem and wept bitter tears of repentance, would have his threefold denial healed by a three-fold declaration of love prompted by the Risen Jesus at that ecstatic breakfast on the shores of the Sea of Galilee. The Risen Jesus who commissions Peter "to feed my sheep" also warns his disciple that the time would come "when you grow old, you will stretch out your hands, and someone else will dress you and lead you where you do not want to go" (John 21:18). The narrator observes: "He said this signifying by what kind of death he [Peter] would glorify God" (21:19).

---

4. See 1 Cor 8:1-13.

5. See the thoughtful ecumenical reflection on the role of Peter in Markus Bockmuehl, *Simon Peter in Scripture and Memory: The New Testament Apostle in the Early Church* (Grand Rapids, MI: Baker Academic, 2012).

The kind of mediating "administrative" role exercised by Peter is also on display in other great characters of the New Testament. One of the figures in the early Church that I greatly admire is Barnabas. He is first introduced in the Acts of the Apostles as an exemplary member of the community, a Levite from Cyprus who "sold a piece of property that he owned, then brought the money and put it at the feet of the apostles" (Acts 4:36). Barnabas was obviously trusted by the leadership of the Jerusalem community and seems to have had the gift of mediation. He is the one who takes Paul under his wing when the still-feared former persecutor and now zealous convert makes his first visit to Jerusalem. Barnabas escorts him before the leadership so that Paul can present himself to them. Apparently the Jerusalem Church still had its doubts about Paul so he is sent home to Tarsus in present day Turkey to cool off. Later it would be Barnabas who goes and retrieves Paul and brings him to Antioch where, after some time in preparation, he will partner with Paul during the first great westward missionary journey (see Acts 13:1-3).

Earlier, echoing the mediating role of Peter with Cornelius, Barnabas was sent by the Jerusalem leaders to see what was happening in Antioch when shocking news had reached them that some Jewish Christians from Cyprus and Cyrene had dared to baptize Gentiles in that major Roman city (Acts 11:19-26). When he arrived, Barnabas determined that what was happening was due to the "grace of God" and instead of condemning the bold stroke of incorporating Gentiles in the community, "he rejoiced and encouraged them all to remain faithful to the Lord in firmness of heart" (11:23). The narrator of Acts adds the comment: "for he [Barnabas] was a good man, filled with the holy Spirit and faith" (11:24). Later, when word of a famine reached the leaders, they once again turned to Barnabas, this time along with his partner Paul, to bring relief from Jerusalem to those who were suffering in the area of Judea.

Barnabas also played a key role in the Jerusalem Council. Both Paul and Barnabas come to the council to defend the Gentile mission of the Church and to counter those Jewish Christians who were demanding that Gentile converts had first to be circumcised (Acts 15:1-2). After Peter had made his decisive intervention in favor of the Gentile mission, the assembly listened to the report of Paul and Barnabas about the success of their first missionary journey in the Gentile world of Asia Minor (15:12). When the council concluded, the apostles and elders send Barnabas as one of the representatives to bring the good news of the council's decision to the Gentile communities in "Antioch, Syria, and Cilicia." The council's official letter refers explicitly to "our beloved Barnabas" (15:25).

Thus, Barnabas, like Peter himself, played a key leadership role within the early community, helping to keep a potentially divided community together and also helping the community finds its way under new circumstances. Barnabas was trusted because he was obviously working for the common good.

Despite his mediating skills, Barnabas shared another experience that Peter, too, had encountered—he clashed with Paul's sometimes fierce perspective! Although Paul and Barnabas, along with John Mark, forged the first missionary team, they eventually had to break up! Setting out on their second missionary journey into Asia Minor, Paul refused to have John Mark join them because he had apparently "deserted" them in Pamphylia and left the team. Their differences could not be resolved so Paul and Barnabas separate, with Barnabas taking John Mark with him and Paul setting off with his new missionary partner, Silas (Acts 15:36-41). Then, as now, the Christian community was a genuinely human community!

A Host of Leaders . . .

The great New Testament historian Martin Hengel once observed that the rapid spread of early Christianity was due not simply to the compelling power of a great idea but to the compelling witness of great people.[6] Many of those great witnesses exercised organizational leadership on behalf of the newly formed Christian community. Aquila and Priscilla, for example, were a Jewish-Christian couple who had been expelled from Rome under the persecution of the Roman emperor Claudius and took up leadership in the Corinthian community. They were there to welcome Paul when he first arrived from Athens (Acts 18:1-4). Paul refers to them as leaders of one of the house churches in Corinth (1 Cor 16:19). So much did Paul prize this couple that he brought them with him to work in the Christian community of Ephesus (Acts 18:18-19). While there, they also took aside the zealous but uninformed Apollos, a new Christian convert from Alexandria, and instructed him more deeply about the faith he was preaching! (18:26). Paul gives them the highest praise for their leadership in his letter to the Romans: "Greet Prisca [an affectionate diminutive for "Priscilla"] and Aquila, my co-workers in Christ Jesus, who risked their necks for my life, to whom not only I am grateful but also all the churches of the Gentiles" (Rom 16:3-4).

Paul also praises Phoebe, a leader of the community at Cenchreae, the small seaport that serviced the city of Corinth. Paul identifies her as "our sister" and "deacon" of this local church and asks that the Roman community would "receive

6. Martin Hengel, *The Charismatic Leader and His Followers* (New York: Crossroad, 1981).

her in the Lord in a manner worthy of the holy ones, and help her in whatever she may need from you, for she has been a benefactor to many and to me as well" (16:1-2). It is clear that Phoebe was an important leader of the community, a woman of some means, and a strong collaborator and supporter of Paul and his ministry. Many scholars believe that in fact Paul had entrusted to Phoebe the delivery of his letter and had sent her to Rome to help secure resources for his planned trip to Spain.[7]

Along with such great community leaders such as Peter, Paul, Barnabas, James, Phoebe, and Aquila and Priscilla, there are scores of unnamed leaders referred to in various New Testament books such as "elders" (the Greek word, *presbyteroi*), "overseers" (the Greek word *episkopoi* from which would be derived the English term for "bishop"), "deacons," and "widows" (some of whom apparently had formal administrative roles in the early community). While we do not have information about the job descriptions of these various administrators, we can infer that holding the community together was an important part of their function. The qualities listed for these roles spell out virtues of stability, common sense, discipline, honesty, integrity, and good management. Thus 1 Timothy declares that a candidate for the role of "overseer" (*episkopos*) should be

> irreproachable, married only once, temperate, self-controlled, decent, hospitable, able to teach, not a drunkard, not aggressive, but gentle, not contentious, not a lover of money. He must manage his own household well, keeping his children

7. See the discussion in Robert Jewett, *Romans*, Hermeneia (Minneapolis, MN: Fortress Press, 2007), 22–23.

under control with perfect dignity, for if a man does not know how to manage his own household, how can he take care of the church of God. . . . He must also have a good reputation among outsiders, so that he may not fall into disgrace, the devil's trap. (1 Tim 3:2-7)

Conclusion: Servant Leadership

We can now draw a first set of conclusions from this brief review of examples of leadership in the New Testament.

1. The inspiration for all leadership in the New Testament is rooted in the example of Jesus. His qualities of compassion, integrity, and selfless service in the carrying out of his mission are reflected in the virtues lifted up in the examples of early community leaders such as Peter, Barnabas, Paul, and Priscilla and Aquila.

2. The fundamental responsibility of New Testament leaders is to foster the common good of the community—and here, too, the example of Jesus is paramount. Jesus the healer and teacher was committed to the restoration and well-being of God's people. So, too, the charismatic leadership of Paul and the more administrative type of leadership exercised by Peter, Barnabas, Phoebe, and Priscilla and Aquila and many others were directed to building up the Body of Christ.

One of the most respected descriptions of leadership, especially leadership exercised in a religious or not-for-profit institution, is the notion of "servant leadership" promoted by Robert K. Greenleaf. Greenleaf considered himself not a theorist about leadership and management but a "practitioner."

He believed that the most effective leader was the "servant leader." In contrast to the prevailing culture that emphasized "watch out for number one," servant leaders "put others first"; where the prevailing institutional culture would strive for the "survival of the fittest," servant leaders say, "We are all in this together." Where the prevailing culture says, "Never trust anyone," servant leaders "trust everyone unless, and until, they prove themselves untrustworthy"[8] Greenleaf also emphasized that the person who aspires to servant leadership must choose first to be a "servant" and then later to be a "leader." In other words, the vocation to service, to reaching out to others in need rather than being absorbed by one's own needs and ambition, is the crucial starting point for this kind of leadership.

The practice of such leadership has evident qualities, Greenleaf observed. The servant leader cares for others and knows his or her followers. He or she is attentive to their needs, is able to listen, provides a vision for the institution, is able to build strong relationships with others, is humble and not threatened to empower others, has a sense of humor, knows how to smile, and strives to build a sense of community.[9]

Above all, Greenleaf emphasized that the ultimate goal of such servant leadership is to help institutions thrive so that through their mission they can contribute to the good of society. Through the mission of these institutions, genuine "service" is extended to our world in desperate need of a more caring and just society.

8. Robert K. Greenleaf, *The Servant as Leader* (Westfield, IN: The Robert K. Greenleaf Center, 1991).

9. See Robert K. Greenleaf, *The Power of Servant Leadership*, ed. Larry C. Spears (San Francisco: Berrett-Koehler, 1998).

It is not difficult to see that the qualities and spirit of leadership that Greenleaf has identified fit comfortably into the New Testament vision of leadership we have been illustrating. The preeminent servant leader is Jesus himself, and those are the very terms he uses in the key saying in Mark 10:45: "For the Son of Man did not come to be served but to serve and to give his life as a ransom for many." Remarkably, Greenleaf did not consider himself a religious person and had only a glancing acquaintance with the New Testament and Christianity. His ideal of servant leadership was fashioned by his altruistic sense of serving the common good through institutions dedicated to caring for society. Yet his notion of "servant leadership" captures the very spirit of Jesus' own exercise of leadership and radiates from examples of leadership found throughout the New Testament. Leadership expressed in service to others is a truly Christian vocation, one at the heart of the Gospel message.

3

Mission and Planning

Robert Greenleaf's emphasis on the vital capacity of religious and not-for-profit institutions to create a more caring and just society in a fractured and violent world brings us to two interrelated and key dimensions of institutional leadership: mission awareness and planning.

Keeping One's Mind and Heart on the Mission

One of the essential responsibilities of the leaders of any institution is that of mission awareness. This is certainly true of those charged with the governance of an institution and is one of the most important responsibilities not only of senior leadership but also of all those who participate in the administration of an institution. Knowing the specific mission of an institution and being dedicated to its fulfillment are crucial for the well-being and effectiveness of any institution—certainly for a religious one. What is our fundamental purpose? Why do we exist as an organization or institution? What impact does our institution intend to have on society? What are the values and fundamental principles that flow from our stated mission and therefore must be incorporated in the way we operate?

Not long ago I was asked to make a presentation at a retreat day for the development department of a major archdiocese. The entire staff was there: the director of the department, the senior development officers for the annual fund and major giving, and the clerical staff, including the receptionist at the front desk. The moderator of the retreat proposed an exercise where each person there—no matter what their level of service in the department—would state how what they did on a daily basis reflected the mission of the archdiocese. It was a fascinating and fruitful exercise. Those who directly approached donors asking for support of the school system or for Catholic Charities had little trouble relating their fund-raising work to the Church's mission of education and serving the poor. But I was also struck by the comment of the receptionist who said that with every person she greets and every phone call she answers, she tries to treat the person with respect and care so that they would know from the very first moment they were dealing with the Church of Jesus Christ. There are always some people in an institution that seem oblivious to the mission and greater purpose of the organization they work for—this woman was not one of them!

As anyone knows who has been involved in the process of formulating or revising a mission statement for an organization or institution, it can be an arduous and even contentious task. A lot is at stake. To be successful and genuine, the statement of an institution's mission must involve all of its stakeholders, have clarity about the institution's history, and consensus about its essential purpose. Then there is the task of finding the right words to express the mission. Some institutions make it a point to have a succinct form of their mission statement visible for everyone to see—on their official publications and annual report, on their website, framed and mounted on the walls of the institution's buildings. This is a wise practice—but even more important is that awareness of the mission of an institution be imprinted on the minds and hearts of the people who make up the organization or institution. There are some institutions that fail to express any formal mission statement at all, but even those that do, if they lose sight of their mission, can drift away from their vital purpose. History, past and present, is littered with defunct corporations and not-for-profit institutions that either went astray and forgot their essential purpose or neglected to adapt that mission to the evolving circumstances of the world they were meant to serve.

The Biblical Roots of "Mission"

We should not forget that even though it has a valid secular connotation, the notion that an institution has a "mission" has deep biblical roots. When a Christian organization or institution reflects on its "mission" it cannot avoid the profound resonances of this term with the fundamental purpose of the Christian mission to the world. Like the Church itself, a Christian institution cannot exist simply for its own well-being but must contribute to the life of the world it is called to serve.

The word "mission" comes from the Latin verb *mittere*, "to send." To have a "mission" is to be "sent" for a specific purpose. In biblical Greek the root word for "send" is *apostello*. From this verb obviously comes the term "apostle"—one who is sent on a mission. The verb form "to be sent" is used 129 times in the New Testament, mainly in the gospels and the Acts of the Apostles, in most instances referring both to Jesus' own mission as one "sent from the Father" and that of his disciples sent by Jesus himself. The noun form "one sent" (i.e., an "apostle") is used seventy-nine times, the vast majority in the Acts of the Apostles and in Paul's letters.

It is clear that being true to one's mission is a fundamental and widespread impulse of Jesus and the early Church. For Jesus himself, this was a central conviction. He was sent by God, by his "Father," to bring renewed life to his own people Israel. Matthew's Gospel makes this explicit. When the "Canaanite" woman urgently asks Jesus to heal her daughter, Jesus instinctively states his mission: "I was sent only to the lost sheep of the house of Israel" (15:24). Only because of the persistent faith of this Gentile woman does Jesus extend his mission beyond the perimeters of Israel. Earlier Jesus had expressed this same unerring sense of his God-given mission to Israel when commissioning the apostles in the Mission Discourse of chapter ten of Matthew's Gospel: "Jesus sent out these twelve after instructing them thus, 'Do not go into pagan territory or enter a Samaritan town. Go rather to the lost sheep of the house of Israel'" (Matt 10:5-6). At the climax of the gospel, the Risen Jesus would send his disciples into the whole world—thus Matthew's Gospel ends with the so-called "great commission"—giving the post-Easter community its fundamental mission of extending the mission of Jesus himself not only to the people of Israel but also now to "all nations" (Matt 28:16-20).

John's Gospel repeatedly refers to Jesus as the "one sent" by God, beginning with the poetic prologue of the Gospel that traces the entrance of God's Word into the world, culminating in the Word becoming "flesh" in the person and mission of Jesus (John 1:14). The whole Gospel of John is, in effect, a reflection on the mission of Jesus whom God's love sends into the world—in the beautiful words of the gospel's first discourse—not to "condemn the world, but that the world might be saved through him" (John 3:17). Some forty-three times in the Gospel of John, Jesus refers to himself as one "sent" by the Father! Jesus' teaching, his healing touch, his confrontation with evil, and, above all, his laying down of his life for his beloved—are all presented as expressions of Jesus' mission to the world.

John's Gospel also emphasizes that the mission of Jesus' disciples is to reflect the character of Jesus' own mission. In his final prayer on the eve of his death, the Johannine Jesus acclaims to his Father, "As you sent me into the world, so I sent them into the world" (John 17:18), a commission repeated by the Risen Christ to his disciples gathered in Jerusalem: "As the Father has sent me, so I send you" (20:21).

What John's Gospel expresses in a succinct formula, the other gospels and the Acts of the Apostles illustrate in manifold ways. During the lifetime of the earthly Jesus, the disciples are sent out to heal and cast out demons in the same manner as Jesus' own mission (see Mark 3:13-19; 6:7-13; Luke 9:1-6). In Matthew's Gospel, the apostles are also commissioned to carry out the mission of Jesus but, unlike in Mark and Luke, they do not actually go out on mission until the very end of the gospel (see Matt 10:5-42). The entire span of the Acts of the Apostles describes the widening mission of the early community, first in the mission activity of Peter and the Jerusalem apostles, and then later in the dynamic mission journeys of Paul and his companions. The foundation of that mission is laid in the final instruction of the Risen Jesus when he is about to depart from them and send the Spirit upon them. Jesus' own mission of proclaiming "repentance and forgiveness of sins" would now be carried out by his disciples and "preached in [Jesus'] name to all nations, beginning from Jerusalem" (Luke 24:47). That commission is taken up again at the beginning of the Acts of the Apostles: "But you will receive power when the holy Spirit comes upon you, and you will be my witnesses in Jerusalem, throughout Judea and Samaria, and to the ends of the earth" (Acts 1:8). Luke, the author of the Acts of the Apostles, takes his story of the unfolding mission of the community to Rome, where Paul, though under house arrest, continues to preach the Gospel "with complete assurance and without hindrance" (Acts 28:31). In other words, the mission of Jesus carried out through the preaching and healing of the apostles and early missionaries continues into history unabated.

This is obviously the case with Paul of Tarsus, whose writing makes up a quarter of the New Testament. This "Apostle to the Gentiles" never tired of reminding his communities that he was one sent by God on mission—i.e., an "apostle of Jesus Christ" (see, for example, Paul's explicit references to his status as an "apostle" chosen and sent by God, placed at the beginning of most of his letters: e.g., Rom 1:1; 1 Cor 1:1; 2 Cor 1:1; Gal 1:1; 1 Thess 2:3-4). Paul's letters are filled with his missionary spirit, a spirit that carried him over ten thousand miles during his lifetime and brought him from Antioch to cities throughout Asia Minor and ultimately to Macedonia, to Greece, and to Rome itself.

Mission as a "Call"

From the biblical point of view, one's mission is rooted in a "call." Thus the notions of "mission" and "vocation" are interrelated. In the gospels, there are several accounts of Jesus' "calling" his disciples and giving them their "mission." In the opening scenes of Jesus' ministry in both Mark and Matthew, Jesus encounters fishermen on the shore of the Sea of Galilee and calls them to "follow him" and to become "fishers of people" (see Mark 1:16-20; Matt 4:18-22). There is no preparation for these encounters—no account of any introductions or conversations. The emphasis is clearly on the majestic authority of Jesus himself who calls Peter, Andrew, James, and John—they respond without hesitation. Later in the gospel story, Jesus will also call Levi the tax collector (called "Matthew" in Matthew's Gospel) to join him—again, the response is without hesitation. Levi leaves behind his tax or toll booth and follows Jesus (Mark 2:13-17).

Luke has a beautiful variant on these first call stories (Luke 5:1-11). Jesus' first encounter with Peter and his associates also takes place along the seashore but in different circumstances. While preaching to the crowds fanned out along a cove of the Sea of Galilee, Jesus is forced to step into a boat moored near the shore in order to have room to address the crowds. The boat happens to be that of Simon. When Jesus finishes preaching, he asks Simon to "put out into deep water and lower your nets for a catch" (5:4). Simon mildly protests, "Master, we have worked hard all night and have caught nothing, but at your command I will lower the nets" (5:5). When they do let down the nets they are rewarded with an abundant catch, one so big it threatens to tear the nets and sink the boats. When Simon sees the abundance, he falls to his knees: "Depart from me, Lord, for I am a sinful man" (5:8). But Jesus reassures Simon—along with his partners James and John: "Do not be afraid; from now on you will be catching [people]" (5:10). And so they, too, followed him without hesitation.

These dramatic call stories have deep roots in the Bible. A whole line of great leaders of Israel receive a "call" from God to take up a mission on behalf of Israel, from the call of Abraham to leave his homeland and set out for a new life (Gen 12:1-3) through Moses at the burning bush called to lead the people out of slavery (Exod 3:4-14), to the mysterious voice that summons Samuel in the night (1 Sam 3:1-21), to the commissioning of prophets such as Amos (7:15-16) or Jeremiah (1:4-8) or Isaiah (6:1-8). The common thread that runs through all of these call stories in both the Old and the New Testaments is that the mission to serve God's people is authorized and finds its roots in God's own care for his people. Ultimately it is God who calls one to serve.

In Catholic tradition, the term "vocation" was often used exclusively to refer to the call to priesthood or religious life. More recent theology has properly realized that all Christians through their baptism are called to serve the mission of the Church to the world. This was explicitly signaled in *Lumen Gentium*, Vatican II's Dogmatic Constitution on the Church. Rather than begin with a description of the hierarchical structure of the Church, the council fathers first described the calling and mission of the whole people of God (LG 9–17). More recently, Pope Francis, in his exhortation *Evangelii Gaudium* (The Joy of the Gospel), has emphasized that all Christians are called to carry out the Church's mission of evangelization: "In virtue of their baptism, all the members of the People of God have become missionary disciples (cf. Mt 28:19). All the baptized, whatever their position in the Church or their level of instruction in the faith, are agents of evangelization, and it would be insufficient to envisage a plan of evangelization to be carried out by professionals while the rest of the faithful would simply be passive recipients."[1]

---

1. Francis, *Evangelii Gaudium* (The Joy of the Gospel), par. 120.

While the term "vocation" can be applied to an institution or organization, it seems more appropriate to consider "vocation" as applying to the personal "calling" of an individual who serves within the mission of an institution or organization. From a Christian vantage point, one can conceive of one's work in a service organization not simply as a "job" but as an expression of our Christian calling to serve the people of God in a worthy and practical manner. I remember seeing a poster on the wall of the Catholic Relief Services headquarters in Amman, Jordan, where a number of young Americans were at work in difficult circumstances: "CRS is not a job but a mission!" A parish, a school, a hospital, a social service organization has a "mission" rooted in the fundamental Gospel mission of bringing life to the world, a mission that is an extension of the mission of Jesus Christ. A person who is committed to the mission of such an organization can authentically see their everyday work as a response to a call from God, a call rooted in their baptism where the power of God's Spirit was granted to them.

Recalling the profound biblical roots of the notion of mission and vocation means that attention to the mission of an institution is not simply a dictate of common sense nor derived from the need to have a coherent and efficient organization. Every effective human organization, from the Rotary Club to the US Military, from Microsoft to the corner grocery, needs to understand its purpose and stay true to its "mission." But for the Christian who is involved with an institution explicitly dedicated to the mission of the Church in whatever fashion that might be, attentiveness to mission has a deeper foundation in the very mission of Jesus, God's Word to the world. For such an institution, an awareness of its participation in the sacred mission of the Risen Christ calls for reflections such as,

"How does the mission of my institution relate to the ongoing mission of proclaiming the Gospel?" "How are such Gospel values as respect for human life and dignity, a commitment to the common good, the virtues of compassion and mercy and justice, expressed in the purpose and operations and environment of my organization?" And for those who work in such an organization, "How is my particular role a genuine expression of my vocation as one called by Christ through baptism to be of service to the world?" "How am I as one involved in the work of administration responding to my call to follow Christ?" "How, through the work I am doing, am I responding to Christ's call for me to be a "witness" to the world?" Standing behind the language of an institution's specific mission statement needs to be this more fundamental purpose and call.

The Mission and the Need for Adaptive Change

There is another lesson about mission that can be learned from its biblical roots. While the fundamental mission of every Christian institution should have continuity with the ongoing mission of Jesus Christ to the world, this does not mean that mission is a static reality. The articulation and implementation of an institution's mission must be adapted to the changing circumstances of the world it is called to serve. Without such adaptive change, an institution can lose its way.

The need for adaptive change is also a part of thoughtful "worldly" wisdom found in many contemporary studies about the mission of institutions.[2] Changing circumstances and

---

2. See work of Ronald A. Heifitz, *The Practice of Adaptive Leadership: Tools and Tactics for Changing Your Organization and the World* (Cambridge, MA: Harvard Business Press, 2009).

new technological advances can have a profound impact on an organization's mission. Ask the Kodak Company what the digital age did to a company whose chief product was film for cameras, or what happened to the Polaroid Corporation, whose founder Edwin Land had invented the Polaroid camera that was hailed as a highly innovative product of its time but was eclipsed by digital photography and finally went out of business. Or think of the challenge to a major retail company like Sears Roebuck that before the age of the Internet depended on the mail-order catalogue for a huge share of its business. Or consider the person in a major American city who has no cell phone and searches for a phone booth to make an urgent call.

Adapting the mission to changing circumstances was also a major challenge for the early Church. As the Acts of the Apostles and Paul's own letters make clear, the Jewish-Christian community struggled to understand the full scope of the mission entrusted to it by the Risen Christ. At first the Jerusalem-based community, composed almost entirely of Jews who had come to believe in Jesus as the Messiah and Son of God, thought that to be a true follower of Jesus meant that one had to first be Jewish. Therefore they expected any Gentile proselyte who wanted to join the community to first be circumcised and to accept the demands of kosher dietary laws and other requirements of the Law of Moses. They firmly believed that this was God's will.

But rapidly evolving circumstances challenged this understanding of their mission. Drawn by the rich sense of community that characterized the early Church and its emphasis on healing and compassion, many Gentiles were ardently seeking to join the Christian community. This influx of Gentiles seems to have already been signaled in the gospels through

Jesus' own encounters with Gentiles such as the centurion of Capernaum (Matt 8:5-13; Luke 7:1-10), the Syro-Phonecian woman from the region of Tyre and Sidon (Mark 7:24-30; Matt 15:21-28), the tortured demoniac of Gerasa (Mark 5:1-20), and the curious Samaritan woman who met Jesus at the well (John 4:4-42). In each case, these Gentiles come to Jesus to seek his help.

In the Acts of the Apostles, Luke notes the alarm of the Jerusalem community when some Greek-speaking Jewish Christians from Cyprus and Cyrene go to Antioch and dare to preach the Gospel to Gentiles and to receive many of them in the community (Acts 11:19-26). The troubled Jerusalem leaders send Barnabas to check out the situation and he reports that what has happened in Antioch was the work of the Spirit of God! A similar shock is experienced by Peter himself. The description of Peter's encounter with the Roman officer Cornelius at Caesarea Maritima is presented by Luke as a major turning point in the history of the earliest Christian community (see Acts 10–11). While napping before lunch in the port city of Joppa, Peter has a dream in which God invites him to eat nonkosher foods. Peter protests that he has "never eaten anything unclean in all my life," but God declares to the confused apostle that "what God has made clean you are not to call profane" (Acts 10:14-15). At that point, emissaries from Cornelius knock on the door of the house where Peter is staying and request that he come to Caesarea, the seat of the Roman Imperial government in Palestine, to speak to his whole household. Peter goes and while he is telling the story of Jesus to Cornelius and his family, the Spirit falls upon them and they become believers. Peter himself is amazed and begins to understand that the scope of the mission he had presumed to understand needed to be expanded: "In truth, I see that

God shows no partiality. Rather, in every nation whoever fears him and acts uprightly is acceptable to him" (Acts 10:34-35). Peter's actions trouble the leadership in Jerusalem and he is called on the carpet. Peter explains what had happened and concludes, "If then God gave them [i.e., the Gentiles] the same gift he gave to us when we came to believe in the Lord Jesus Christ, who was I to be able to hinder God?" Peter's testimony sways the Jewish-Christian leaders who begin to see the light! "When they heard this, they stopped objecting and glorified God, saying, "God has then granted life-giving repentance to the Gentiles too" (Acts 11:18).

This remarkable story, which covers two whole chapters of the Acts of the Apostles, clearly shows how the early community had to change its perspective and adapt its mission as it encountered new and unanticipated realities. The earliest Jewish-Christian followers of Jesus had apparently not expected that Gentiles would become a significant part of the Christian community. This was a sea change that would demand a host of adaptations for the early Church as it moved further out into the Mediterranean world. Luke describes the Council of Jerusalem in chapter 15 that brings together the leaders of the Jewish-Christian community, such as Peter and James, and those who were carrying the mission to the Gentile world, such as Barnabas and Paul. After deliberation, the leaders accept the success of the mission to the Gentiles and confirm the work of such missionaries as Paul and Barnabas and their companions. What is proposed at the council, according to Luke, was something of a compromise: Gentiles were to be accepted into the community without the imposition of circumcision, but they were asked to keep the kosher diet and not to marry within the family blood lines dictated by Jewish law.

This accord did not erase all of the problems and challenges for the early Church as it adapted its mission to the Gentile world. While Luke sees the compromise solution of the Jerusalem Council as a smooth adaptation, Paul seems to have had a different perspective. In his letter to the Galatians, for example, Paul strongly protests those Jewish Christians who are attempting to subvert his work by dogging his footsteps and demanding strict observance of the Jewish law on the part of his Gentile converts. At the same time, Paul also reports his bitter disappointment in Peter who in Antioch at first shared table fellowship with Gentile Christians but then had withdrawn from such meals under criticism from Jewish-Christian representatives who had come from Jerusalem (Gal 2:11-14).

What is clear from many other references in the New Testament is that it took the early Church some time and experimentation to fully adapt its mission in order to embrace the Gentile world. Thus their mission—although rooted in the life-giving mission of Jesus himself—was not static but needed to be adapted to new circumstances in order to retain its vitality and to be true to its ultimate purpose of bringing God's life to the world.

The adaptation required was not only about membership. As the community grew and became more complex, it also had to develop organizational structures that would enable the community to be sustained.[3] The Acts of the Apostles tells us that the first generation of Jerusalem Christians met in their homes and went together to the temple for prayer and liturgy (Acts 2:43-47). That structure could not work for the increasing number of Christian communities outside of Jerusalem. Evidence from Paul's letters, for example, reveals

3. See above, chap. 1, esp. pp. 16–19.

that small groups of Christians met in private homes where they prayed together and celebrated the Lord's Supper (for example, 1 Cor 11:17-34). Later on, the early community would outgrow this type of structure, too, and begin to adapt existing basilica-type buildings for gatherings of the community and later still to build places of worship specifically designed for that purpose. An interesting example of such expansion can be found in Capernaum, where a room in a home—probably that of Simon Peter—was gradually expanded and then totally reconstructed to serve as a Byzantine church.

There is no doubt that the organizational structure of the Church also grew and adapted to new circumstances. More loosely organized and more charismatic type leadership structures at the outset gave way to a more developed formal structure involving local leaders such as "overseers" (*episkopoi*), "elders" (*presbyteroi*), "deacons" (*diakonoi*), and "widows" (*cherai*). The early Church rapidly organized a communication system among local churches—something that became crucial in order to maintain a level of unity. A communications system included circulation of letters and messages from leaders to local churches, travelling apostles and teachers who maintained catechetical instruction among the Christian communities, the convening of important meetings such as the council mentioned in Acts 15, a system of providing financial support for missionaries (see Paul's expression of thanks to the Church at Philippi for their support; Phil 4:15-20) and for local congregations (for example, Paul's elaborate collection for the sake of the poor of the mother church of Jerusalem; see 1 Cor 16:1-4), and the relief organized by the Jerusalem Church during a famine in Judea (Acts 11:27-30).

Such adaptation of the Church's mission and its structures has continued throughout history. In the wake of the

Enlightenment, the Church struggled to come to grips with modernity, at first rejecting it wholesale and only over time making necessary adaptations. The work of the Second Vatican Council can be seen as a major effort to adapt the Church's mission to the rapidly changing circumstances of the world in the wake of World War II and the major changes that have swept the modern world. That adaptation continues to this day, not without conflict and controversy, but still occurring in order to give new vitality to the ongoing mission of the Church. What is true of the Church as a whole is also obviously true of those organizations and institutions that make up the Church worldwide. Without thoughtful change and adaptation, the eternal mission of the Church could atrophy and weaken.

Mission and Planning: Setting One's Face toward Jerusalem

Being true to the mission of an institution also requires planning for its future. The necessity of strategic planning is stressed in virtually every discussion about effective administration. Even though we have no crystal ball, schools of theology and seminaries have to think about the evolving mission of the Church, the kinds of conditions our students will face in the years ahead, and how best we can prepare them now for the future they are likely to see. A diocese, synod, or parish has to think of the demographic shifts that might take place in the community it serves and how that will affect the needs for schools and other institutions. Hospitals and social service agencies have to think about future financial trends in the complex and rapidly evolving world of health care. And, of course, we all know that planning cannot be a sporadic activity if it is to be effective. An institution has to constantly be in a planning mode if it is to survive, and much of the responsibility for this falls to those in administration.

And here, too, I believe our biblical heritage has a lot to say to us. Planning is not just a necessity imposed by common sense but, like the notion of mission itself, has deep roots in our biblical and theological heritage. The whole Bible tilts toward the future. In fact, the entire ethical teaching of the Bible could be summed up in the formula: striving to live now by the future we most earnestly desire to see. Israel longed for the Promised Land, and when its own social and political experience proved possession of the land to be transitory, it began to long for God's definitive *shalom*, for the advent of God's reign that would bring lasting peace and justice. Jesus stood in this tradition and his entire ministry was a proclamation of God's coming reign and the call to live now in the light of that experience. The Beatitudes become one powerful expression of that future vision. So, too, do Jesus' parables of the kingdom, in which merchants sell all in the hope of acquiring an infinitely valuable pearl and the treasure seeker risks everything to buy the field where the greatest prize of all lies buried and waiting.

But institutional planning, like anticipation of the reign of God, is not idle speculation or whimsical anticipation of possible future joy or accomplishment. To move an institution and its resources toward the future required by its mission takes great effort and is one of the most demanding of administrative responsibilities. In the latest version of the accreditation standards of the Association of Theological Schools of the United States and Canada, schools of theology are exhorted to think through together their common mission and so be prepared to do the adaptive work necessary to face the future in a healthy manner. It sees this as the core responsibility of an institution and its leadership.

Here, too, the realism of the biblical imagery is worth our reflection. I think in a particular way of Luke's Gospel and his second volume the Acts of the Apostles. From my own experience of trying to work with colleagues to think about the future and to act with the needed discipline and foresight to anticipate it, I found myself reading Luke in a new way. Luke wants to demonstrate to his readers how the life and mission of the Church emerged from the past history of Israel and the mission of Jesus himself. Hence the Acts of the Apostles follows upon the gospel story. Jesus' teaching and ministry, his formation of a community of disciples, and his faithful perseverance in his mission creates the possibility for the gift of God's Spirit that will be ultimately lavished on the Church and ignite its mission to the world. Jerusalem, in the setting of Luke's overall narrative, becomes both the endpoint of Jesus' earthly mission and the starting point for the mission of the community.

So Jesus "sets his face" toward Jerusalem, in Luke's memorable phrase (Luke 9:51). "Setting one's face toward Jerusalem"—the very words reflect Luke's emphasis on the determination, the discipline, the fidelity needed for Jesus to complete his mission. Jesus' teaching at this point in the gospel drives that lesson home. Would-be disciples are warned not to look back or to turn their heads to other concerns. "Let the dead bury their dead," Jesus declares (Luke 9:60). Jesus' parables are likewise sober on this point of preparing for the future: would a king go out to oppose an opposing king's army without first seeing if he has the resources to face his enemy (Luke 14:31-33)? Would someone intending to build a tower not first sit down and estimate the cost to see if he has enough resources to complete it rather than risk ridicule for starting something and not being able to finish it (Luke 14:28-30)? So the disciples are to think of what it takes to carry out their mission and ensure that they have the commitment and resources to do so. To this extent, the work of planning and the discipline needed to bring the whole community's attention to that task is an exercise of Christian hope and Christian responsibility for the future.

The Grace of Unwelcome Realities

As important as planning is, it does not solve everything. Some of the most difficult and most life-giving realities for me and for the institution I served were unplanned and often unwelcome. Change comes to institutions in complex and unexpected ways. Several years ago I heard Donald Shriver, the former long-term president of Union Theological Seminary in New York, interviewed about his experience as president. What had been the most important thing he needed to do his job well, he was asked. I have never forgotten his reply: "the spiritual discipline needed to face unwelcome realities."

Surely dealing with unwelcome realities is not a special preserve of those who serve in administration, but I tend to think the job of an administrator brings a healthy dose of them. I realized that as an administrator I never really knew what was coming through the door next: an unexpected personnel problem, a pressing financial crisis, a burst steam pipe and a big repair bill, someone resigning or ill that you had counted on, the disruptive intervention of some event or person you had not even thought of. Every administrator could recite experiences that sometimes take our breath away or exhaust our enthusiasm.

But sometimes the unwelcome realities are not painful problems or losses but simply unanticipated circumstances or sudden opportunities that throw us and our carefully laid plans off track. And so we have to go back to the drawing board. A few years ago we were planning to renovate and expand our existing venerable facilities in order to find room for our expanding student body. We consulted with a noted architect who pointed out the practical hurtles for such a move and the fact that it would cost more to do our planned renovation than to actually build something new. At first this news was a blow to our expectations, and we continued to explore ways we could adapt our current building, but, over time, after a lot of false starts and impractical proposals, the excitement of creating a new academic center on our campus made us forget our earlier plans!

Such experiences could be chalked up to chance, but from a deeper Christian perspective, they can also be seen as moments of grace. Here, too, the biblical precedents are illuminating. As noted earlier, a most instructive passage for mission and planning is the story of Peter and his meeting with Cornelius in Caesarea Maritima, as Luke presents it in chapters 10 and 11 of the Acts the Apostles. Peter, on a rooftop in Joppa and enjoying the noonday sun before lunch, had a dream that would change his life and that of the early Christian community forever. What up to that point had been a purely Jewish-Christian community would now begin to open its portals to Gentiles who eagerly sought to join this community. Things would never be quite the same!

In fact, the whole story of the Jerusalem apostles is one of constant surprise, as the Spirit outruns the Church and confounds its expectations. So much of the Bible is that way—God at work in discontinuity, God's presence found in unexpected people and in unexpected circumstances. Even

Jesus himself seems to experience this in his encounter with the Canaanite woman (see Matt 15:21-28), when his initial refusal even to speak to this Gentile woman finally yields before the unrelenting assault of her faith. The fixed expectations of a traditional "Israel first" theology have to give way to the unexpected and apparently unwelcome determination of the Canaanite woman on behalf of her daughter.

Such examples in the Bible prompt us to ask: where is the Spirit to be found? Surely God's Holy Spirit is found in the leaders of the community and in the normative teachings and actions of the community. But these examples, and in fact the entire Biblical saga, remind us that the Spirit of God is not confined to Israel or to the Church but roams the world and works through events and people we might never anticipate.

Think of the saga of Israel—from one perspective, it is an amazing catalogue of how events that on the surface seem random and hardly sacred shape the movement of God's people through history. For example, a search for grazing lands brings Abraham to the land of Israel, just as a strange mix of deadly family rivalry leads to the exile of Joseph and hard-pressed famine in turn leads Jacob and his sons to seek refuge in Egypt. These seemingly random events set in motion the remote history of Israel. Slavery and oppression from an Egyptian despot sets the stage for the Exodus. And when the Promised Land is finally reached and Israel appears to conquer the land, it in turn is shaped by so-called pagan culture already present there, adapting as its own the language, the architecture, and even the religious rituals of the Canaanites.

Israel eventually adopted a monarchical form of government and law codes that echoed those of other ancient Middle Eastern civilizations. Israel's adoption of a monarchy derives from secular experience, yet it ultimately gives Judaism and

Christianity the language for our messianic hopes in referring to the "Messiah," or one anointed as king, as well as the strong metaphor of anticipating the onset of the kingdom or reign of God. Exile imposed by Assyrian and Babylonian oppression becomes a key to Israel's spirituality. The invasion of Alexander the Great brings Hellenistic culture into the biblical heritage and provides the language of our gospels and many of the categories and concepts that make our Christology possible. Christianity breaks out of the confines of Palestinian Judaism not only because of the inherently centrifugal dynamics of the Gospel but also because the Jewish revolt of AD 66. This revolt and the brutal Roman suppression of it would change both Judaism and Jewish Christianity forever.

We know this story continues. The people who built the huge religious buildings to serve as novitiates and seminary buildings in the fifties and sixties that some now have to wrestle with never dreamed that a sea change would come only a few years later and sweep everything in front of it. The shape that priesthood, ministry, and Church will take in the future will be influenced just as much and more by the shifting platelets of culture as they will by our discussions, documents, and good faith planning efforts. Are these the accidents of history or the tyrannies of fate? Or is the Spirit of God also at work in these profound and often surprising shifts in history and culture? We should not forget Gamaliel's principle, first told to the Sanhedrin of Jerusalem in the fifth chapter of the Acts of the Apostles: "If this endeavor or this activity is of human origin, it will destroy itself. But if it comes from God, you will not be able to destroy them; you may even find yourselves fighting against God" (Acts 5:38-39). Thomas Aquinas put it another way: all truth, wherever it is found, is from the Holy Spirit. And that Spirit, the Bible tells us, ranges far and wide on the horizons of the world and sometimes makes its presence felt in unexpected ways.

These examples could be multiplied. The Bible views the world as an interface of chaos and order. Within that schema, the administrative role is to help bring order and predictability and due process to the life of a community through adaptation of the institution's mission and by thoughtful planning. But there has to be room for chaos to enable order to be established—room for the unexpected, for the prophetic, for the new and unanticipated. It does take spiritual discipline, a spiritual detachment, to allow room for God's prophetic spirit to shake our ordered securities. But by being attentive enough to search for the stirrings of God's Spirit in the unexpected and even the unwelcome realities we face, we also find the strength and imagination to adjust and seek new life. Jesus' final advice to his disciples on the eve of his death was to "stay awake" (Mark 13:37). One cannot predict when the moment of God's grace would break in the world, and so one had to be alert and ready.

Similarly, one wise trustee who served on our board and who had long experience in leading a university reminded me that a strategic plan could never fully anticipate the future—the future will bring its unexpected surprises—but the exercise of careful planning does enable an institution and its leadership to be prepared to respond to such surprises when they happen. Good planning alerts us to the realities of the evolving world we serve and reminds us of the resources we need to face our future, even if it comes in an unexpected form.

Conclusion

Stewardship of an institution requires attention to its mission, the willingness to do the adaptive work to keep that mission alive, and the need to plan thoughtfully and realistically for its future. Such work is not simply smart corporate practice but, in the context of Christian faith, is a response to a God-given call to serve the world as Jesus himself did. The administrative leaders who help an institution remember its mission and plan for its future fulfill the words of Jesus to his disciples: "Every scribe who has been instructed in the kingdom of heaven is like the head of a household who brings from his storeroom both the new and the old" (Matt 13:52); i.e., something "old" by remembering and being faithful to one's mission; something "new" by being willing to adapt that mission to changing circumstances and by being open and ready to respond to what the future may bring.

4
Community in the Workplace

If you search the Internet on the topic "community in the workplace," you will encounter hundreds of articles and books. Experts concerned about the need for productivity and satisfaction in the corporate world have discovered that a sense of "community" is an important factor. Yet in a lot of other sectors of modern society, a sense of community seems to be eroding. Robert Putnam touched a chord in his now famous image of "bowling alone," suggesting that American individualism was overriding a sense of community.[1] In many sectors of American society, there is a loss of community—less cohesion in neighborhoods, the isolation of the nuclear family from its extended network, a diminishment of the local church as the focus of religious and social community activities, and so on. A deep current of our society emphasizes the autonomy of the individual as a prime value. This is a genuine value, but it can have an underside: a sense of loneliness and isolation.

1. See R. Putnam, *Bowling Alone: The Collapse and Revival of American Community* (New York: Simon and Schuster, 2000).

The Workplace and Community

But one place that people are still brought together is the workplace. Nearly half of the waking hours of most people's lives are taken up with their job. The workplace is usually not the primary community of an employee; one hopes that family and friends come first, and for many others, their parish or congregation still remains a vital source of community support. If someone begins to consider their place of employment as their primary experience of community, it can often lead to a distortion in one's life—being all consumed with work. While some companies may speak of their employees as a "family," that designation does not quite fit. Families, for example, don't hire or fire their members, and if an administrative leader considers him or herself as a "parent," one can expect most employees to chafe under such a paternalistic perspective. Yet at work, people can find meaning and purpose for their lives. In the community formed at the workplace, they can experience shared values, mutual support, and even genuine friendship with their colleagues. It is not a surprise that a lot of office romances spring up and even blossom into marriage.

Writings on this subject readily identify the kind of virtues that promote a sense of community and satisfaction in the workplace: civility and respect, a shared purpose, mutual encouragement and care for others, a sense of responsibility and accountability, appreciation for creativity, fairness and transparency, and an environment that is inclusive—welcoming those of diverse backgrounds and cultures. An institution or organization that prizes this kind of work environment places a high value on its employees as human beings and is not concerned only about efficiency or productivity. Not surprisingly, time after time studies have shown that a workplace with a healthy sense of community is more productive and efficient than those where a sense of community is absent.

Community within a Religious Organization

Here, as in the other components of institutional life we have considered—leadership, mission, and planning—our Scriptures and our Christian heritage bring a particular richness and wisdom to the kind of working environment that should characterize a religious institution or organization. Fashioning the workplace into a community is, in fact, another way that the vocation of administration can be an expression of one's Christian commitment. The workplace is neither our family nor our church—but the perspectives and virtues we bring to our work should flow from the deepest levels of our commitment as followers of Jesus.

Perhaps the best analogy for a sense of community in the workplace might be the quality of community expected of the Church itself. The New Testament avoids identifying the Church simply as a "family." Although some New Testament writers readily address their fellow Christians as "brother" or "sister," these are used as terms of endearment to express the bond that ties Christians together. Paul and other New Testament writers also speak of the Church as a "household"; but the extended family of the first-century Greco-Roman world, which included slaves and other extended family members, was more like a small institution or cottage industry and very different from the nuclear family of the Western culture of the twenty-first century.[2] When speaking of the Church as a whole, other nonfamilial models are used. This is reflected in several gospel stories where Jesus speaks of his true "family"

---

2. See David Balch and Carolyn Osiek, *Early Christian Families in Context: An Interdisciplinary Dialogue* (Grand Rapids, MI: Eerdmans, 2003); also Margaret Y. MacDonald, *The Power of Children: The Construction of Christian Families in the Greco-Roman World* (Waco, TX: Baylor University Press, 2014).

as not his blood family but as the community of his disciples. In the Gospel of Mark, for example, when Jesus is informed that his mother and his brothers were outside of the house where he was teaching and asking for him, he replies: "Who are my mother and my brothers?" And then looking at the circle of disciples sitting around him, he said: "Here are my mother and my brothers! . . . Whoever does the will of God is my brother and sister and mother" (Mark 3:31-35; see similar passages in Matt 12:46-50 and Luke 8:19-21).

In other words, the community of Jesus is not formed along blood lines or based on the hierarchy of parents and children but develops according to discipleship lines. Those who do the will of God are the true "family" of Jesus.

A related text is found in Matthew 23:9, in which Jesus instructs his disciples, "And call no one your father on earth, for you have one Father—the one in heaven." In the community of Jesus, no one is a "parent" but all are disciples (that is, "learners") of the one Father. For the early Church, a sense of egalitarian discipleship was more fundamental than bloodlines. This was particularly important in the context of early Christianity where in Greco-Roman society the head of the patriarchal family had dominant authority over the entire household, even determining the friendships, religious ties, and the social associations of his spouse, his children, and his slaves. As indicated in the First Letter of Peter, this social context of the family made it very difficult for women and slaves to be able to join the Christian community if their husband or master did not approve.[3] Moving away from the model of the family and

---

3. The author of 1 Peter admonishes the wives of non-Christian husbands (those "who do not obey the word") to win them over "without a word" but through the "purity and reverence" of their lives (see 1 Pet 3:1-2).

basing kinship among Christians on "doing the will of God" also facilitated the opening to the Gentiles. Membership in the Christian community was not based on one's ethnic background or religious status but on one's response to the Gospel.

Thus the New Testament views the Church as a community of disciples, finding the foundation of their common life in their faith in Jesus and building a sense of community that reflected Jesus' teachings and example. While family life was, of course, prized as a genuine expression of Christian existence, with the relationships between spouses and between parents and children reflecting Gospel values, the community itself was thought of in more egalitarian terms as a community of equals. In this sense, the Christian community or "church" can serve as a certain model for the workplace.

The Qualities of a Christian Community: The Example of Jesus

The specific qualities that should characterize relationships within the Christian community are found throughout the New Testament. Ultimately the nature of the Christian community is based on the teaching and example of Jesus himself. In the Sermon on the Mount, for example, Jesus urges the disciple, if offended, to check one's anger, to refrain from insult, and instead to seek reconciliation with one's brother or sister (Matt 5:21-26). One's word is to be honest and truthful: "Let your 'Yes' mean 'Yes,' and your 'No' mean 'No'" (5:33-37). There should be no retaliation for injury: "When someone strikes you on your right cheek, turn the other one to him as well" (5:38-42). And, in one of the most remarkable teachings of Jesus, the disciples are urged to love even their enemies—in so doing they reflect the great mercy and compassion of God who "makes his sun rise on the bad and the good, and causes rain to fall on the just and the unjust" (5:45).

Later in Matthew's Gospel, in what is called the "community discourse," Jesus again instructs his disciples about the qualities of a genuine Christian community. Here Jesus seems to be speaking to the leaders of the community and describing the kinds of attitudes that reflect the Gospel. Thus the leaders should be humble like a child (18:2-5), should care for the vulnerable members of the community—seeking them out rather than despising them (18:6-14)—resolve conflicts in a reasonable and respectful way (18:15-20) and, above all, have a spirit of unlimited forgiveness (18:21-35). John's Gospel characteristically condenses Jesus' teachings about community into the memorable phrase: "Love one another as I have loved you" (John 15:12).

Jesus' teaching reflects the manner of his own life. His entire mission is characterized in the gospels as a giving of life for the sake of the other. In a key passage in Mark's Gospel where Jesus and his disciples are on their fateful journey to Jerusalem, Jesus draws a sharp contrast between the way the imperial authorities dealt with people and the way power was to be exercised in the Christian community. "You know that those who are recognized as rulers over the Gentiles [i.e., the Roman imperial authorities] lord it over them and their great ones make their authority over them felt. But it shall not be so among you. Rather, whoever wishes to be great among you will be your servant; whoever wishes to be first among you will be the slave of all" (Mark 10:42-44). Jesus concludes with a profound statement about his own life and mission: "For the Son of Man did not come to be served but to serve and to give his life as a ransom for many" (10:45). All of his life—his healings, his association with the outcasts and the vulnerable, his words of inspiration and comfort, his confrontation with injustice, his care and feeding of the poor—all of this was an act of "service" (the Greek word, *diakonia*), an outpouring of Jesus' life on behalf of all.

Thus Jesus' teachings on the qualities of an authentic Christian community were, in effect, a description of the qualities of his own life. And here again John's Gospel succinctly expresses the ultimate meaning of all this. Jesus' entire mission was an act of self-sacrificing love. On the eve of his arrest, Jesus told his disciples: "No one has greater love than this, to lay down one's life for one's friends" (John 15:13). In fact, John's Gospel declares that the ultimate source of Jesus' mission was God's own love for the world that prompted him to send his Son for the sake of the world: "For God so loved the world that he gave his only Son, so that everyone who believes in him might not perish but might have eternal life" (3:16). Later Christian theology would reflect on the awesome reality that the taproot of all Christian sense of community was the very life of the Trinity—that community of mutual and infinite love that constitutes the mystery of God's own being.

Paul and Community

Drawing on Jesus' teaching and example, specific exhortations about the qualities of a Christian community are found throughout the New Testament. This is especially true in Paul's letters, as he dealt with factions and divisions within the various Christian communities with whom he was engaged. One strong example is found in Paul's letter to the Philippians, a community he had founded on his first missionary trip into Macedonia and for which he had deep affection. The Philippian Church was vibrant but apparently also had some sharp divisions. Two of its prominent women members—Euodia and Syntyche—

seemed to be embroiled in a public dispute (see Phil 4:2-3). So at the outset of the letter, Paul makes an earnest appeal for harmony: "If there is any encouragement in Christ, any solace in love, any participation in the Spirit, any compassion and mercy, complete my joy by being of the same mind, with the same love, united in heart, thinking one thing. Do nothing out of selfishness or out of vainglory; rather, humbly regard others as more important than yourselves, each looking out not for his own interests, but everyone for those of others" (Phil 2:1-4).

What is key for understanding Paul's thought is what comes next. The apostle turns to the example of Jesus himself: "Have among yourselves the same attitude that is also yours in Christ Jesus"—and here Paul quotes what was probably an early Christian hymn that may have been known to the Philippians as well—"Who, though he was in the form of God, did not regard equality with God something to be grasped. Rather, he emptied himself, taking the form of a slave, coming in human likeness; and found human in appearance, he humbled himself, becoming obedient to death, even death on a cross. Because of this, God greatly exalted him and bestowed on him the name that is above every name, that at the name of Jesus every knee should bend, of those in heaven and on earth and under the earth, and every tongue confess that Jesus Christ is Lord, to the glory of God the Father" (Phil 2:6-11).

This magnificent hymn poetically portrays Jesus, whose being is divine, "humbling" or "emptying" himself for our sake. He left behind his divine majesty and endured the cross out of love in order that humans might thrive. Theologians have referred to this process of "emptying" oneself for the sake of others as "kenosis"—derived from the Greek verb "to empty" oneself found in the hymn which is also translated as "humbled himself." It is this process of "kenosis"—self-transcending love for the sake of another—that is the foundation of all Christian community. This is the basis for Paul's exhortation to the Christians at Philippi to put aside their differences and deal with each other in a spirit of mutual respect, forgiveness, and love.

One of Paul's most famous passages on this subject is his description of charity in chapter 13 of his first letter to the Corinthians. The run-up to this beautiful text is important. Throughout the letter, Paul is disturbed about factions that have divided the Corinthian community (see, for example, 1 Cor 1:10-17). He is particularly upset about a report he has received concerning the conduct of some members of the community at the celebration of the Lord's Supper. The Christians gather for this sacred meal in a large home or villa that can accommodate the community. After the formal prayers of the ceremony, the participants share a meal. But Paul is distraught that instead of the meal being a sign of unity, it has become a way of accentuating differences—the wealthy eat and drink well while the poor members go hungry (1 Cor 11:17-22). Paul seems to pull out all the stops in confronting these deep and painful divisions in the community. He reminds them of the origin and meaning of the Lord's Supper as a commemoration of Jesus' own life-giving death (1 Cor 11:23-26). He goes on to speak of the community as united in one Spirit but having a multitude of gifts that are to work in harmony (1 Cor 12:4-11). In one of his most famous images for the Christian community, Paul describes the community as the very "Body of Christ"—with all the members being vital parts of the one Body of Christ, each mutually dependent on the other and caring for the other (1 Cor 12:14-31).

This entire span of Paul's letter reaches its climax in his "hymn to charity" (1 Cor 13:1-13). Perhaps no more beautiful description of Christian love has ever been formulated. For all its beauty, the qualities mentioned by Paul have a practical and realistic flavor—reflecting the genuine experience of those who strive to love another:

> If I speak in human and angelic tongues but do not have love, I am a resounding gong or a clashing cymbal. And if I have the gift of prophecy and comprehend all mysteries and all knowledge; if I have all faith so as to move mountains but do not have love, I am nothing. If I give away everything I own, and if I hand my body over so that I may boast but do not have love, I gain nothing.
>
> Love is patient, love is kind. It is not jealous, [love] is not pompous, it is not inflated, it is not rude, it does not seek its own interests, it is not quick-tempered, it does not brood over injury, it does not rejoice over wrongdoing but rejoices with the truth. It bears all things, believes all things, hopes all things, endures all things.
>
> Love never fails. If there are prophecies, they will be brought to nothing; if tongues, they will cease; if knowledge, it will be brought to nothing. For we know partially and we prophesy partially, but when the perfect comes, the partial will pass away. When I was a child, I used to talk as a child, think as a child, reason as a child; when I became a man, I put aside childish things. At present we see indistinctly, as in a mirror, but then face to face. At present I know partially; then I shall know fully, as I am fully known. So faith, hope, and love remain, these three; but the greatest of these is love.

Paul was convinced that the ability to forge a genuine Christian community depended on the power of the Holy Spirit lavished on the community through the death and resurrection of Jesus. The apostle draws a sharp contrast between what he calls "the works of the flesh" and "the fruits of the Spirit." The term "flesh" for Paul did not mean simply our physical body but a self-centered perspective that was self-indulgent and oblivious to others' needs—the very opposite of the spirit of Jesus himself. In listing the "works of the flesh," it is obvious that Paul was thinking in particular of problems in living out a community life. Along with such culprits as "impurity," "drinking bouts," "orgies and the like," Paul also lists "hatreds, rivalry, jealousy, outbursts of fury, acts of selfishness, dissensions, factions, occasions of envy" (Gal 5:20-21). By contrast, the "fruits of the Spirit" are the very virtues that create a genuine sense of community: "love, joy, peace, patience, kindness, generosity, faithfulness, gentleness, self-control" (Gal 5:22).

Similar exhortations about community are found in virtually all of Paul's letters and in other New Testament texts.[4] The Letter to the Ephesians is something of a summary of Paul's theology, probably written by a later disciple of the apostle. It has a beautiful exhortation about community: "I, then, a prisoner for the Lord, urge you to live in a manner worthy of the call you have received, with all humility and gentleness, with patience, bearing with one another through love, striving to preserve the unity of the spirit through the bond of peace; one body and one Spirit, as you were also called to the one hope of your call; one Lord, one faith, one baptism; one God and Father

---

4. Such exhortations abound in the New Testament. See, for example, Rom 12:9-21; 15:5-6; 1 Cor 12:31–13:13; 2 Cor 13:11-12; Eph 4:1-16, 31-32; 5:18-20; Phil 4:8-9; Col 3:5-17; 1 Thess 4:9-12; 5:11, 12-22; 2 Tim 2:22-26; Heb 13:1-16; 1 Pet 3:8-9; 4:7-11. Jesus' own words about forgiveness play a prominent role in the Sermon on the Mount: e.g., Matt 5:21-24, 43-48; 6:12, 14; see also the emphasis on forgiveness in the so-called "community discourse" of chapter 18 (18:21-35).

of all, who is over all and through all and in all" (Eph 4:1-6). The Letter to the Hebrews, written to encourage a community under duress, also has a beautiful exhortation to charity: "Let mutual love continue. Do not neglect hospitality, for through it some have unknowingly entertained angels. Be mindful of prisoners as if sharing their imprisonment, and of the ill-treated as of yourselves, for you also are in the body" (Heb 13:1-3).

The First Letter of Peter has a particularly rich notion of Christian community. The author is convinced that the cohesion and mutual love that should characterize the community can serve as a witness to the surrounding non-Christian culture. Thus the letter urges the Christians to "be of one mind, sympathetic, loving toward one another, compassionate, humble. Do not return evil for evil, or insult for insult, but, on the contrary, a blessing, because to this you were called, that you might inherit a blessing" (1 Pet 3:8-9). The author returns to this motif near the end of the letter in one of its most beautiful passages: "Above all, let your love for one another be intense, because love covers a multitude of sins. Be hospitable to one another without complaining. As each one has received a gift, use it to serve one another as good stewards of God's varied grace. Whoever preaches, let it be with the words of God; whoever serves, let it be with the strength that God supplies, so that in all things God may be glorified through Jesus Christ, to whom belong glory and dominion forever and ever. Amen" (1 Pet 4:8-11).

Implications for the Workplace

This sampling of New Testament texts demonstrates how important a spirit of genuine community was to the early Christians as they attempted to follow the teachings and example of Jesus himself. While the ideals expressed in these texts may seem exalted, the exhortations themselves clearly reflect a very human gathering, striving to overcome the challenges that community life always brings; hence the repeated references to avoid quarrels, contentions, jealousy, envy, dissension, etc.—the culprits known to any group of people who attempt to forge a community in whatever setting that may be. While many of these lists of vices and virtues are reflected in the writings of first-century non-Christian authors speaking about society itself, for Christians the motivation and strength to form a community and to work in harmony and as "one body" were rooted in the deepest wellsprings of their Christian faith.

Thus when it comes to building a sense of community in the workplace, our Christian heritage supplies a powerful motivation and an abundance of practical wisdom. The effort to forge an authentic spirit of community in the workplace is, from the Christian perspective, not simply an effective way to reduce workplace stress and to increase productivity—even though these are documented outcomes of a genuine community spirit. For the Christian dealing with fellow workers with respect and care, avoiding toxic rivalries and jealousy, asking for forgiveness when someone has been offended, seeking to be dedicated and accountable in one's work—all of these virtues become a practical expression of one's Christian vocation of bringing the witness of the Gospel to the world in which we live. This should be particularly true of institutions whose mission is rooted in the Gospel: Christian hospitals, schools, parishes, social service agencies, and the like. How strange it would be to have an institution bearing the name Christian yet having a workplace environment that was anything but Christian. The workplace of any institution, including expressly Christian ones, should not be confused with a church or a monastery. Almost always such institutions include employees who may not be Christians or who do not prefer to think of their everyday work as some sort of ministry. They should not be coerced into a religious frame of mind. Yet all, including those without an express religious motivation, can benefit greatly from a working environment that is suffused with the virtues that also characterize the Christian sense of community.

Communication and Speech

An important but sometimes underrated ingredient for building community is the quality of our speech and communication skills. In my experience, a constant concern of the people who make up any institution is the need for good communication. Communication has to be built on a commitment to transparency on the part of the leadership and key personnel of any institution. Some information, of course, requires discretion and limited public knowledge, e.g., an employee's compensation, a sensitive personnel problem, perhaps an idea that first needs to be aired by key governance bodies before being circulated more widely. But beyond these obvious examples, information that helps everyone be aware of the institution's mission and policies, as well as key decisions about its direction, should be communicated to everyone involved. This is a natural corollary of having mutual respect and a sense of community. Withholding important information or deliberately leaving someone "out of the loop" is a surefire way to create resentment and divisions in the workplace.

Leadership and Language

Choosing the right words and the right images to use in dealing with an institution's mission and the challenges it may face is also a subtle but important part of leadership. Should the decision to eliminate a specific program be viewed and discussed as a symptom of retrenchment or failure? Or is it more accurately and constructively described as a necessary adaptation of an institution's mission to changing times? Is a reorganization of internal structures to be approached cynically as shifting the deck chairs on the Titanic? Or should such a change be recognized as a good faith effort to be more efficient and accountable for the sake of our mission? Is the initiation of a new program or position a reckless waste of resources? Or should the proposed innovation be discussed as an act of fidelity to the institution's core mission? Finding the right words to describe what an institution is facing is a vital act of leadership. The "right words" cannot be superficial or mask a problem but must reflect the truth in a constructive and perhaps even an inspiring way. Many institutions have found their initiatives stalling because some people decide at the outset to set a negative tone and use cynical ways of describing what, in fact, is a positive step for an institution's vitality.

One of my most vivid memories about the impact of being truthful and transparent with my colleagues came during the so-called "Great Recession" of 2008. Like many other institutions, this sudden and severe economic downturn had a very negative impact on our budget. In order to maintain our economic equilibrium we had to take some radical, if transitory steps: cut backs on spending, deferring hirings and pay raises, even for a time having to introduce some furloughs among our staff. Our executive team had weighed all the options facing us and decided not to cut staff—since so many of our loyal staff and their spouses were themselves facing economic crises at home. But we did have to make painful choices in other parts of our operation. While I was confident we had made the right decisions, I also realized that many of our staff and faculty were fearful of what was going to happen. I decided to call a "town meeting" of all our faculty and staff and to explain as completely and openly as I could what we were facing as an institution, what were the options available to us, and what we were intending to do. The atmosphere was tense as the meeting got underway and there were a number of pointed questions and comments raised about the situation. I found myself speaking very earnestly and with no little feeling about the challenges we were facing. At the same time, I communicated with confidence that together we could meet those challenges. At the end of our session—much to my utter surprise—those assembled stood and applauded! I realized they were not applauding me but expressing their support for CTU as it faced a serious situation. Having access to all the facts and hearing the solution that was being proposed gave them confidence in what was going to happen and the courage to undertake it. That was a lesson in the value of open communication I would not soon forget!

Institutions also need clear and effective communication with their essential external publics. Public relations need not be seen as some sort of gimmick or crass propaganda. Most religious institutions depend in a serious way on the support of the wider community in order to carry out their mission. People will give to institutions and causes they trust and value. Effectively communicating the mission of an organization or institution and demonstrating the good that it does is, in fact, keeping faith with the people whose vital support keeps the mission alive.

How We Speak to Each Other . . .

Another dimension of the issue of speech and communication is the quality of our discourse with each other within the organization. The natural virtues of courtesy and civility, of speaking respectfully and in a friendly manner with each other, are also virtues that reach deep into our Christian heritage. To address a fellow employee in harsh or mocking terms, to fail to greet them in the corridor or even to learn their name, to spread noxious gossip about someone—these are behaviors that work against a spirit of community and drain the joy out of a workplace. This is particularly important for those in leadership. A sarcastic or angry word from a major administrator to another employee cuts deeply and often leaves a lasting wound. This is especially so if a sharp word from an administrator is spoken in public. There were a few times in my experience when a sudden gust of anger led me to speak sharply to a colleague; I always regretted doing so and felt that those sharp words were lingering in the mind and heart of that same colleague for a long time afterward.

The New Testament Witness

It is no accident that the New Testament, which places such a premium on forging genuine communities, gives strong attention to the quality of our speech.[5] Here again the example of Jesus is the foundation. In the Sermon on the Mount, for example, one of the first instructions Jesus gives is to avoid speaking to a brother or sister in angry and contemptuous language such as calling them "*raqa*" (a colloquial term which meant "imbecile" or "blockhead") or "fool" (Matt 5:22). Later in the same sermon, Jesus tells his disciples that their speech should be honest and transparent: "Let your 'Yes' mean 'Yes'

5. Some of the material in this section on the issue of speech in the New Testament is adapted from Donald Senior, "'Speaking the Very Words of God,' New Testament Perspectives on the Characteristics of Christian Speech," in *Between Experience and Interpretation: Engaging the Writings of the New Testament*, ed. Mary F. Foskett and Wes Allen (Nashville, TN: Abingdon, 2008), 35–52.

and your 'No' mean 'No'" (Matt 5:37). In a controversy with his opponents about ritual purity, Jesus enunciates a fundamental principle: it is not what goes into a person's mouth that contaminates them (i.e., eating "unclean" food) but what comes out of the mouth and originates from the heart—namely, "evil thoughts . . . false witness, blasphemy" (15:19). In another such passage, Jesus severely warns the religious leaders: "A good person brings forth good out of a store of goodness, but an evil person brings forth evil out of a store of evil. I tell you, on the day of judgment people will render an account for every careless word they speak. By your words you will be acquitted, and by your words you will be condemned" (12:35-37).

The Letter of James

This attention to the way we speak to one another is found throughout the New Testament. The most extensive treatment is found in the Letter of James. In James 3:1-12, there is a strong warning about the power of the "tongue" which the author compares to the rudder of a ship—a small piece of the overall boat but one that has extreme importance and power. In this spirit, James warns his Christians in 1:26, "If anyone thinks he is religious, and does not bridle his tongue but deceives his heart, his religion is vain." James's strong teaching about speech finds its ultimate rationale in the very nature of Christian existence. He notes the paradox that from the same tongue can come both "blessing and cursing" (3:9-10). The iniquity expressed by the abusive tongue leads to a state of "double-mindedness" (*dipsuchos*; see 1:8; 4:8) that is a fundamental concern of James. The Christian has to be firmly rooted in friendship with God and cannot succumb to the spirit of the "world" which is saturated with evil (see 3:13-18; 4:4-10). Those who are animated by friendship with God express God's wisdom in their lives, namely, they are "pure, then peaceable, gentle, compliant, full of mercy and good fruits, without inconstancy or insincerity" (3:17). By contrast, the one who is a "lover of the world" (4:4) leads a life tainted by a whole series of vices ("jealousy," "selfish ambition," "disorder," "every foul practice"; see 3:16). From such friendship with the world come the cravings that lead humans astray, even to acts of violence (see 4:1-4; the author lists "wars and conflicts").

Such "double mindedness" or split allegiance between God and evil results in the same human instrument—the tongue—expressing both "blessing" and "cursing." James's words express the inherent scandal of this—with the same tongue one blesses "the Lord and Father" and then curses "human beings who are made in the likeness of God" (3:9). As the author exclaims: "Brethren, this need not be so" (3:10). At stake, therefore, is a fundamental integrity that must be present within the being of the Christian. Made "in the likeness of God" and committed to "friendship with God," Christian speech must be in harmony with this overriding reality. The content and manner of one's speech should come from within the depths of one's being as a creation of God and one made in God's own likeness. This perspective underlies virtually all of James's exhortations about the quality of relationship and speech that should pass between the members of the community. The Christians should "humble [them]selves before God" (4:10) and "not speak evil against one another" (4:11). Echoing the saying of Jesus in Matthew 5:37, the word of the Christian needs no external oath to insure its honesty, but a "yes" is a "yes" and a "no" is a "no" (see Jas 5:12-13).

Other New Testament Texts

While the Letter to James contains the most extensive reflections on proper Christian speech and its theological foundation, there are other significant New Testament texts worth considering. Most of these are found in the later, deutero-Pauline materials; this may in fact reflect the increase of doctrinal and other factional disputes within the community—leading to more contentious speech.

In the concluding portion of the Letter to the Colossians, for example, the author turns to exhortation. The theological foundation for Christian conduct is similar to that described in James: through the resurrection of Christ, the Christians are "to think of what is above, not of what is on earth" (Col 3:2). This entails "putting away" such earthly things and avoiding those practices symptomatic of one who lives an "earthly" life such as "anger, fury, malice, slander, and obscene language" (3:8). The community members are also urged "to stop lying to one another" (3:8). By contrast, those who "have put on the new self" (3:10) exemplify "heartfelt compassion, kindness, humility, gentleness, and patience" (3:12). They are to "bear with one another" and "forgive one another, if one has a grievance against another; as the Lord has forgiven you, so must you also do" (3:13). They are to let "the word of Christ dwell in you richly" and therefore "in all wisdom teach and admonish one another, singing psalms, hymns, and spiritual songs with gratitude in your hearts to God. And whatever you do, in word or in deed, do everything in the name of the Lord Jesus, giving thanks to God the Father through him." Noteworthy is the emphasis on the quality of Christian discourse which is not to give way to anger or inappropriate (i.e., "abusive") speech but takes on the specific Christian hues of forgiveness, gratitude, and even a tone of prayer and liturgical praise.

A similar saying punctuates the letter but extends the exhortation of gracious speech to dealings with those outside the community: "Let your speech always be gracious, seasoned with salt, so that you may know how you ought to respond to each one" (4:6). Here the author employs a conventional metaphor "seasoned with salt" which implies speech that is pleasing and appropriate.[6] The Christian is to be ready to answer the questions and challenges of those outside the community and to do it in a manner that reflects the same values that should characterize speech within the community.

As in Colossians, the exhortations to proper speech in the Letter to the Ephesians come as illustrations of the new way of life that expresses the Christians' state before God. The author reminds the Christians that they had been taught "to put away the old self of your former way of life, corrupted through deceitful desires, and be renewed in the spirit of your minds, and put on the new self, created in God's way in righteousness and holiness of truth (Eph 4:22-24). This entails "putting away falsehood" so that the Christians would "speak the truth, each one to his neighbor, for we are members one of another" (4:25).

As in the other texts we are considering, uncontrolled anger is included in the list of behaviors unbecoming a Christian. The Christians are exhorted to "be angry but do not sin; do not let the sun go down on your anger, and do not make room for the devil" (4:26-27). Likewise, "No foul language should come out of your mouths, but only such as is good for needed edification, that it may impart grace to those who hear" (4:29). The author continues (4:31) with similar exhortations that illustrate Christian conduct that flows from a life renewed in Christ, with several of the vices repeating the list of Colossians 3:8: they are "to put away all anger, fury, malice, slander, and obscene language." By

6. See Margaret Y. MacDonald, *Colossians and Ephesians*, Sacra Pagina Series (Collegeville MN: Liturgical Press, 2000), 173, who refers to Plutarch's use of the same metaphor; also James D. G. Dunn, *The Epistles to the Colossians and to Philemon*, New International Greek Testament Commentary (Grand Rapids, MI: Eerdmans, 1996) 266–67.

contrast, they should "put on heartfelt compassion, kindness, humility, gentleness, and patience, bearing with one another and forgiving one another, if one has a grievance against another; as the Lord has forgiven you, so must you also do" (3:32).

Chapter 5 of Ephesians has a profusion of such exhortations, with a strong emphasis on appropriate discourse. In Ephesians 5:4, the Christians are warned that speech that is "obscene," "silly," or "vulgar" is entirely out of place; instead, Christian speech should be characterized by "thanksgiving." As in James and Colossians, characteristic Christian discourse that is prompted by the Spirit should be marked by "singing psalms and hymns and spiritual songs," "singing and making melody to the Lord in your hearts," "giving thanks always and for everything in the name of our Lord Jesus Christ to God the Father" (5:19-20).

The First Letter of Peter has similar exhortations to proper Christian speech but the overall context of the letter and its theology gives it a somewhat different tone from that of Colossians and Ephesians. As in the previous letters, the author is concerned about the cohesion of the Christian community and the proper relationship among the members rooted in the new reality of their Christian existence. But there is also a strong "witness" dimension to the theology of this letter; the author is aware that the communities he addresses lead a somewhat precarious existence as "aliens" and "exiles" in their own land and face mounting misunderstanding and even hostility on the part of the surrounding dominant culture.[7]

7. See the discussion in Donald Senior and Daniel Harrington, *1 Peter, Jude, and 2 Peter*, Sacra Pagina (Collegeville, MN: Liturgical Press, 2003), 7–10; also, Paul J. Achtemeier, *1 Peter*, Heremeneia (Minneapolis, MN: Fortress, 1996), 23–35; John H. Elliott, *I Peter*, The Anchor Bible Yale Commentaries, vol. 37 B (New York: Doubleday, 2000), 87–117.

How they act toward each other and toward their neighbors is a part of a "mission strategy" to present the community in a positive light to the wider community.

This is evident, for example, in the exhortations of 1 Peter 3:8-13. The members of the community are urged to "be of one mind, sympathetic, loving toward one another, compassionate, humble" (3:8). They should not "return evil for evil or insult for insult, but, on the contrary [return] a blessing" (3:9). Presumably the evil and abuse foreseen here are from those outside the community. The author goes on to cite Psalm 34:13-17 and here introduces more explicitly the notion of proper speech. Those who "would love life" are to "keep the tongue from evil and the lips from speaking deceit" (1 Pet 3:10). The Christians should stand ready even in the face of suffering and abuse to give a witness to those outside the community "for your hope" but do it with "gentleness and reverence" (1 Pet 3:15-16).

A final exhortation concerning proper speech is found in 1 Peter 4:11, and it echoes the conclusions of the other letters we have considered where a lyrical description of Christian discourse is given: "As each one has received a gift, use it to serve one another as good stewards of God's varied grace. Whoever preaches, let it be with the words of God; whoever serves, let it be with the strength that God supplies, so that in all things God may be glorified through Jesus Christ, to whom belong glory and dominion forever and ever. Amen" (1 Pet 4:10-11).

The Pastoral Letters of 1 and 2 Timothy and Titus also reflect on the role of speech within the Christian community, particularly on the part of those who teach or lead the community. "Paul"—the proposed author of the letter—urges Timothy to counsel teachers not to be embroiled in "myths and endless genealogies" (1 Tim 1:4) or to engage in "meaningless talk . . . without understanding either what they are saying or what they assert with such assurance" (1 Tim 1:6-7). Rather, the aim of Christian instruction should be love which comes "from a pure heart, a good conscience, and a sincere faith" (1 Tim 1:5). The author returns to this theme at the conclusion of the letter. The one whose teaching is not in accord with the words of Jesus Christ and godliness "has a morbid disposition for arguments and verbal disputes" from which come "envy, rivalry, insults, evil suspicions, and mutual friction" (1 Tim 6:3-4). Leaders and members of the community should not be "aggressive" or "contentious" (1 Tim 3:3). Deacons, likewise, are not to be "double-tongued" (1 Tim 3:8; *dilogos*), most probably a reference to deceitful speech.[8]

Timothy himself should set an example in "speech," as well as in other aspects of his conduct (4:12). He should not speak "harshly" or in an overbearing manner to his elders but "appeal to him as a father. Treat younger men as brothers, older women as mothers, and younger women as sisters with complete purity" (5:1). As a "man of God" he should exemplify "righteousness, devotion, faith, love, patience, and gentleness" (6:11).

Similarly, in 2 Timothy, the author exhorts Timothy to remind teachers to "stop disputing about words" (2 Tim 2:14; cf. 1 Tim 6:3-4) which does no good and leads to catastrophe for the listeners. Idle talk spreads "like gangrene" (2 Tim 2:17). All "foolish and ignorant debates are to be avoided because they only breed quarrels (2 Tim 2:23). The truly Christian teacher, by contrast, is "gentle with everyone, able to teach, tolerant, correcting opponents with kindness" (2 Tim 2:25)—the latter

---

8. See I. Howard Marshall, *The Pastoral Epistles*, ICC (Edinburgh: T & T Clark, 1999), 489.

phrase emphasizing the quality of "kindness" even in dealing with those who are "in opposition."[9]

In somewhat sharper tones, the Letter to Titus warns of the need to silence "rebels, idle talkers and deceivers" (Titus 1:10). Titus is to urge "younger men" to be models of good works and exemplify sound teaching (2:7-8). In a final exhortation (3:1-8) that gathers several of the virtues deemed characteristic of Christian speech, the author exhorts the whole community to be "open to every good enterprise" (3:1) which is demonstrated by not speaking evil of anyone, avoiding quarrels, being gracious, and showing gentleness to every person.

The Foundation and Character of Christian Speech

Although the contexts, literary style, and overall theological perspective of the New Testament texts we have considered each have their own distinctiveness, an overall profile of what is considered a "Christian" manner of speech and its theological basis or rationale is detectable.

1. As elaborated most explicitly and extensively in the Letter of James, the fundamental basis for the quality of Christian speech is found in the very being of the Christian that has been transformed by his or her renewed life in Christ. Because the Christian has been "recreated" or "renewed" by God, they are no longer to live as they may have in their previous way of life. One of the characteristic expressions of this new way of living or transformed life is the manner of one's speech, first and foremost with other Christians but also with those outside the

9. Ibid., 766.

community. The character of one's speech must ultimately reflect the character of one's being before God.

2. There is also consistency in these New Testament passages in naming those qualities or virtues which should characterize Christian speech. Thus Christian speech is not contentious or "bullying" or arrogant but "gentle" and "humble." Christian speech, reflective of Christian life itself, is aimed at building up the community and is therefore loving and forgiving rather than confrontative and destructive. It must be truthful and honest—unadorned and not elaborate or artificial. Certain manners of human speech that are destructive of community relationships are typically avoided: unbridled expressions of anger, slander, quarrels, abusive or obscene speech, useless or idle speech, lying and deceptive speech. Even when it is necessary to be corrective, the Christian is urged to do so with "gentleness" and "compassion." Proper relationships within the community must be maintained by thoughtful and respectful speech; thus leaders should not speak in an overbearing manner; speaking with one's elders should be respectful and considerate. Particularly revealing and uniquely characteristic of these exhortations to proper speech are those that call for the singing of hymns and words of liturgical praise. Given the assumptions about the nature of speech as expression of one's transformed being before God, it is entirely logical that the ultimate expression of Christian speech would be that of prayer and praise of God.

It should be noted that the emphasis on the generally irenic character of Christian speech in these New Testament texts is not incompatible with other more forceful and confrontational rhetoric. Standing within the biblical tradition of prophetic speech and accustomed to polemical forms of debate within the wider Greco-Roman and Jewish cultural contexts of the time, these authors did not hesitate to sharply criticize opponents or to vigorously correct those they had judged to have gone astray. The same could be said, of course, about Jesus' own sayings reflected in the gospel traditions of his encounters with his opponents. Despite this, however, the overall thrust of those texts where these New Testament authors give explicit counsel about the use of speech, the emphasis falls on moderation and constructive forms of discourse.

While the early Christians were no strangers to conflict, both among factions within their communities and with opposing forces outside the communities, nevertheless the exhortations of their normative literature was to use speech that was tolerant, respectful, compassionate, and forgiving. The Christians were, in fact, urged to speak like the God revealed through Jesus Christ.

Dealing with Conflict: Embracing the Crucified Body of Christ

Ask any administrator what causes them their greatest heartache and undoubtedly most will say "personnel issues." Having to confront someone; having to make a decision to "let someone go" as we say; realizing that you have failed to be attentive or fair or considerate to a colleague; or finding yourself the target of chronic antagonism from someone simply because you fill the symbolic role of being in authority—these and other similar experiences often make up some of the most painful aspects of everyday administrative life, and yet they go to the heart of what administrative leadership is all about.

As we noted in the chapter on leadership, the primary work of the administrator is to serve the community as a whole.[10] It is to help create an environment in which the institution can carry out its mission effectively. Some have described this as creating a "holding environment" for the work of an institution: that is, helping provide the right atmosphere, the necessary resources, and an absence of obstacles so that people can carry out their responsibilities in relative peace and security.

It is self-evident that those in administrative leadership have to care for the institution as a whole and not just one part of it. But institutions are not abstract realities. I have come to discover that institutions are fairly mysterious and that they have a life of their own. This is because, fundamentally, institutions are people. Institutions are organized for a certain purpose and equipped with a certain amount of resources and perhaps housed in a physical plant, but most important of all and most evident of all, institutions are made up of people.

This is as true of religious institutions as it is of every corporate structure. Parishes, seminaries, hospitals, social service agencies, diocesan chanceries—people, rather than equipment or facilities, are key. One of the things that I realized when I became the administrator of Catholic Theological Union, a graduate school of theology, was how complex and manifold this community of people really was. Shortly after I was appointed president, I had a meeting with all of our support staff. I was startled to realize—after having served for nearly sixteen years on the faculty—that the staff was as numerous as the faculty. I became aware how little I realized what the contributions of some people on the staff were. I knew my faculty colleagues well. But in most cases I knew little about the personal lives

10. See chap. 2, pp. 40–41.

of the maintenance personnel or the people that ran the food service or the clerical staff. And I soon found myself being the informal chaplain to many of the trustees and their families— people I had hardly known before in my years on the faculty.

And I came to know a lot more about how people interacted and what their foibles and strengths were. I saw people at their best and at their worst. I discovered more of the humanity of some of our faculty and staff than I had ever known—and sometimes, more than I ever wanted to know! I remember the wise comment that Fr. Vincent Cushing, the long-time president of Washington Theological Union, handed on to me from one of his Franciscan superiors: "Don't try to make people happier than they want to be!" While having to deal with the human realities of an institution is everyone's privilege, I have found that those in administration have the opportunity to interact on a daily basis with more of its human dimension than, for example, faculty do. The work of the administrator is plunged into the public and communal dimensions of an institution, having to interact with all of the groups and interests that comprise it.

The Body of Christ

Surely having to work with the community of people that forms an institution—people in all their glory and their shame—involves us in something that is close to the heart of the Gospel. Being an administrator whose responsibility is to care for the community of people that make up such an institution is nothing less than caring for the good of the Body of Christ. We should not confuse a school or other type of religious institution with a family or the Church itself or with some kind of a quasi-religious community. Institutions are not identical with any of these, although they partake of some of their values and dynamics. Yet a school of theology or a parochial school, or a parish community, or a Catholic hospital, is surely one authentic expression of the Body of Christ. It is a coming together of people of faith for the sake of the Gospel, and the relationships that bind together that community can certainly be viewed as an embodiment of the Risen Christ in the midst of God's people.

While one could slip into spiritual rhapsody about the beauty of being the Body of Christ or an authentic form of Christian community, I am struck by the realism with which the Bible anticipates the heartache and hard work necessary to live in and help maintain the Body of Christ, or build it up, as Paul often spoke of it. In more recent years, I have asked myself when I think of the Body of Christ, what kind of a body do I imagine—the Risen Christ as Adonis, with a beautifully developed torso in the manner of classical Greek art? Or when Paul uses that image, is he thinking of the *Crucified* Body of Christ? I think one can make a strong case that Paul has in mind the Christian community as the Crucified and broken Body of Christ. Whenever Paul speaks of his own body, he cites its "weakness"; it is an "earthen vessel" (2 Cor 4:7), a body that carries within it the death of Jesus (2 Cor 4:10). Surely Paul's own turbulent relationship to the Corinthian Church reflects that perspective. By the time Paul arrives at chapter 12 of his first letter to the Corinthian Christians, where he uses this provocative symbol to describe the community, he had already addressed a host of ripe problems in the Corinthian Church: bitter and rival factions, lawsuits, incest, sexual promiscuity, divorce and remarriage, and chaos during the liturgy, to name a few. So when Paul applies the image of the Body of Christ to the Corinthian Church, he is not describing an ideal community but a real community, one broken and crucified. Perhaps this is why he speaks about honoring the weaker members of the body and giving them greater dignity, about not being tempted to cut off a part of the body that might seem repulsive or useless (1 Cor 12:22-23).

And the gospels, too, portray Jesus and his teaching realistically, anticipating how demanding is the work of reaching out for the strays and keeping everyone at the table when trying to fashion a Christian community. The good shepherd has to leave the wholesome flock and trek after the stray who is determined to go off on his own (Matt 18:12-14). One suspects that the stray had probably played this role a few times. And think in this connection about the exquisite realism of Jesus' parable of the prodigal son where the father has to temper his joy over solving a problem with one troubled and straying son in order to deal with the resentment of the other son who never left and who complains that he is neglected (Luke 15:11-32).

And how about the way all four gospels portray the community of the disciples—a community chosen by Jesus and privileged to live in his presence? Yet Jesus' band of disciples is hardly an ideal community, displaying remarkable ignorance, seldom reacting with heroism or grace under pressure, and ultimately denying, abandoning, and betraying Jesus in his hour of greatest need. The mood of the gospel story about the disciples is a sadder but wiser mood, a community at best reconstituted after monumental failure and weakness. Frankly, as an administrator, now more than ever acutely aware of one's own weakness and seeing that same mortality in the community I served, this portrayal of the disciples of Jesus was a comfort.

For many readers of the New Testament, Paul's description of his confrontation with Peter in Antioch when, under criticism from some in the community, Peter withdrew from table fellowship with Gentiles, seems a bold and a heroic support for the gospel of freedom. Yet as an administrator, I felt great sympathy for Peter. What was it like to have to mediate between, on the one hand, James, the brother of the Lord, and the strongly traditional circumcision party in Jerusalem who were shocked to see Gentiles entering the community without the restrictions of the Jewish law, and, on the other, with Paul of Tarsus, who wanted the Gentiles to be completely free of the law and was always pushing out the margins of the community? The compromise hammered out at the Council of Jerusalem in Acts 15 is a Petrine compromise and one that probably reflected the historic role of Peter as a mediator between some of these conflictual currents in the early community.

Perhaps later in his career—and I am only speculating here—Paul may have felt more sympathy for Peter when he, too, had to be the mediator and reconciler within his own communities. After all, if we can believe Luke's account in Acts, Paul, along with Barnabas, had the honor of being the first Christian missionary team and the monumental embarrassment of being also the first one to break up in an argument! It reminds me of the story of the first two people in town to own a Model T who then end up running into each other!

In any case, the effort to serve the community as a whole, the energy it takes to be equitable and inclusive for the sake of the mission of the institution, the emotional discipline needed to restrain one's own feelings in order to keep peace and maintain one's proper role as a centerpoint within a community's various currents—all of these commitments, I believe, plunge us deep into the heart of the Gospel and the life-giving ministry of Jesus who came not to be served but to serve and to give his life in ransom for the many. Such an exercise of power is truly in the Gospel spirit; it is in the manner of the servant leadership of Jesus, the Good Shepherd.

Paul notes—perhaps somewhat wryly given his stormy relationship with the Christians of Corinth—"But as it is, God placed the parts, each one of them, in the body as he intended" (1 Cor 12:18). Not as we choose, but as God chooses. That is the community we are given to serve and the community for which we are required to give our life force. For example, by working within an academic community that prepares ministers for the Church, I am engaged in a noble profession. I am actually building up the Body of Christ. Not an abstract body, but a real body, even a crucified and broken body—and being an administrator allows me on a daily basis to understand how real that body is, how it has a life of its own.

On Being "Detached"

One of the liabilities of experiencing the community in this way is that it can lead to cynicism or bitterness. I have known more than a few ex-deans, ex-presidents and ex-religious superiors and former pastors who have retired from office feeling cynical and bitter about many of the people and institutions they had served.

In a chapter on community in his beautiful and challenging book *Life Together*, Dietrich Bonhoeffer warns that something to be avoided in attempting to live in community is to fall prey to "dreaming."[11] We are not called to live in a dream world but in the real world. One symptom of such "dreaming," he notes, is to be scandalized at the realities of a less than ideal

11. Dietrich Bonhoeffer, *Life Together: A Discussion of Christian Fellowship* (New York: Harper and Row, 1954), 26–30.

community. Christian community, Bonhoeffer observes, is not an ideal that we must realize, but rather, it is a reality created by God in Christ in which we must live. Directing a clandestine seminary under the terrible threat of Nazism gave Bonhoeffer's reflections a profound urgency and realism.

Dealing with the realities of a real-life community such as the life of any institution, religious or not, calls for an abundance of patience and serenity, even in the midst of conflict and some emotional turmoil. Administrators who are responsible for dealing with personnel issues also need to "depersonalize" conflicts without, at the same time, becoming "impersonal." Very often personnel issues have little to do directly with the administrator themselves, even when the issue might be framed that way by the aggrieved party. Personnel who are in distress may have other factors in their lives—family issues, self-confidence issues, health issues—that are contributing to their emotional turmoil in the workplace. Some colleagues have deep-seated and chronic problems with those in authority, no matter who they may be.

There is a classic virtue that makes sense here—namely, the virtue of "detachment." "Detachment" in this context means that the person in authority is able to put some space between their own personal well-being and the impact of conflict and dissension that are an inevitable part of an administrator's job. When I first became president of CTU, negative reactions or comments from one of my colleagues would cut deeply, and I would expend a lot of emotional energy pondering where I had gone wrong or working up some anger at what I considered unfair criticism. But over time and with some wise advice from trusted friends, I learned to achieve some emotional discipline and would not take every slight or criticism as a personal setback. I strove to remain committed to my job and to dealing with coworkers fairly and compassionately, but I also learned the importance of the Christian virtue of "detachment."

Seeking Forgiveness

Beyond dealing with one's own emotional serenity, there is another important response to issues of conflict in an institution. A sense of forbearance, patience, a willingness to forgive and seek reconciliation are all germane Christian virtues in dealing with interpersonal conflicts in an organization. But there is something further, namely, insuring that there are equitable structures and consistent procedures in an organization to help either prevent conflicts or deal with them in a prudent and fair way when they occur. Such elements as evaluation and accountability, transparent and equitably applied wage scales, fair and workable grievance procedures, sound personnel policies regarding such things as harassment in the work place—all of these contribute to either reducing conflict or dealing with it in a proper manner.

In the Gospel of Matthew, where Jesus speaks of such beautiful ideas as unlimited forgiveness and loving care for the neighbor, there are also common sense instructions on how to deal with a difficult member of the community. In Matthew 18:15-17, when someone in the community commits an offense, Jesus instructs his disciples to first go and try to resolve things one on one. If that does not work, then the aggrieved party should enlist the help of two trusted members to meet with the offending party and work things out. If that fails, too, and the offense of the errant member is grievous, then they should be expelled from the community. Jesus concludes this instruction on conflict resolution with an interesting comment: once expelled, the errant member is to be treated "as you would a Gentile or a tax collector" (18:17). The question then becomes, how should we deal with "Gentiles and tax collectors"? At that point, one realizes that in the gospel account, Jesus is solicitous and welcoming precisely to people like this! In other words, even though the good of the community may demand serious disciplinary steps, the errant person remains an object of care and potential reconciliation.

Conclusion

Drawing on our biblical heritage and the example of Jesus and the early Christian community, we discover that the art of building up a sense of community in the workplace is not simply a matter of common sense or the desire to experience the efficiency of a happy organization versus one that is divided and sour. Making the daily effort to build a genuine sense of community also reaches into the deepest convictions of our faith tradition and is an important way of bringing the message of the Gospel to our workplace.

5

Finances and Fund-Raising

Dealing with money is an inevitable and crucial part of administrative work, especially for those at the leadership level of an institution. First of all, there is the ongoing effort to secure enough financial support to sustain the institution's mission. Unless an institution has a massive endowment that covers all operating expenses, this translates into fund-raising, with efforts stretching from bake sales at the local parish to major capital campaigns for universities and hospitals. In today's world, few heads of not-for-profit organizations can survive without being willing to ask for financial support.

Along with acquiring adequate financial support, there is the equally challenging aspect of determining how to allocate the financial resources of an institution. The need for more resources seems to cry out from every corner of an institution: for more adequate compensation for staff, for more personnel, for more ongoing maintenance and improvement of facilities, and so on. Here, too, the leadership of an institution has a primary responsibility, but all of the personnel of an institution have to cooperate in the prudent use of an institution's precious resources.

Our goal in this chapter—as throughout the book—is not to provide a minicourse on financial administration or institutional advancement. Educational resources for this are abundant elsewhere.[1] Rather, our goal is to consider how this financial or economic dimension of administrative service is also deeply rooted in our biblical and Christian heritage and how, in fact, meeting the challenge of financial administration is also an expression of a Christian vocation of service.

The "Reluctant Steward"

Compounding the challenge of dealing with the financial or economic dimensions of an institution is the well-documented fact that many of the key personnel of religious institutions are often not comfortable in dealing with financial matters. As noted earlier, the Lilly Endowment conducted a study a few years ago to determine the attitudes of Protestant and Catholic seminarians and pastors toward the responsibilities of fund-raising and administration within the range of their pastoral duties. The results were published under the title *The Reluctant Steward*.[2] As the title indicates, most of the target audience recognized the theoretical importance of such matters but preferred not to have to deal with them. They did not see fund-raising or administrative duties as being at the heart of their pastoral work, nor did they consider them a source of satisfaction. This original study was revisited a decade later and the results were similar. While there had been some improvement, the researchers concluded that the

1. See, for example, John Zietlow, *Financial Management for Nonprofit Organizations: Policies and Practices* (Hoboken, NJ: John Wiley and Sons, 2007); Thomas A. McLaughlin, *Streetsmart Basics for Nonprofit Managers*, 3rd ed. (Hoboken, NJ: John Wiley and Sons, 2009).

2. Daniel Conway, Anita Rook, and Daniel A. Schipp, eds., *The Reluctant Steward* (Indianapolis, IN, and St. Meinrad, IN: Christian Theological Seminary and St. Meinrad Seminary, 1992).

stewards, in this instance Protestant and Catholic pastors and the seminaries and agencies responsible for their academic and pastoral formation are still "reluctant." Many pastors continue to feel awkward and underprepared about fund-raising and the other administrative duties required by their roles. They also still have ambivalence about how to address such "reluctance," admitting that more practical training is needed at the seminary and in-service levels but not having much enthusiasm for such educational experiences themselves. By and large, seminaries and Church judicatories land in the same spot: recognizing this is an important pastoral concern but not quite sure how and where to tackle it.

This ambivalence about the economic or financial dimensions of administrative work is a symptom, I believe, of an underlying problem that explains why many pastoral leaders shy away from talking about money or fund-raising and find little meaning in the administrative dimensions of their ministry. Part of our problem may be that we have not thought through how these practical realities fit into our own vision of Christian life, much less into our roles as ministers of the Gospel or pastoral leaders of Christian communities. We do give proper attention to the more explicitly religious domains such as doctrine, prayer, worship, spirituality, and service and such crucial experiences as marriage and family. But I know that in my own experience, the transition from full-time teaching of Scripture to an administrative role as president was a revelation for me of how little I had thought about financial and administrative responsibilities as part of my vocation as a minister of the Gospel and a theological educator.

The skills necessary for administration of a parish or other religious institution and the willingness to ask for its financial support are not identical, and each has its own requirements and challenges. But diffidence about such tasks may arise from a wider common context, namely, how a religious leader envisions the place such practical realities have in relation to their own Christian life and vocation.

If some involved in religious institutions are reluctant or ambivalent in dealing with financial matters, the same is not true of the Bible and of Jesus himself. The gospels attest that Jesus talked a lot about money. Sixteen of the thirty-eight parables found in the gospels deal with handling money and possessions. Howard Dayton, who has written and lectured extensively on the Bible and finances, claims that "the Bible offers 500 verses on prayer, less than 500 verses on faith, but more than 2,350 verses on money and possessions."[3] I haven't checked these statistics, but it is surely true that the Bible and Jesus himself were not afraid to deal with the singular importance of money and possessions in human life. The Scriptures engage the realities of human life in all its dimensions, including finances as one of the most important. The resources—financial and otherwise—needed to sustain human life are a common concern of everyone who works for a living.

An experience I had a few years ago has become something of a parable for me whenever I think about pastoral leadership and such practical matters as money, fund-raising, and the nuts and bolts of administration. We had a retreat weekend for our board members, and one of the sessions focused on the profile of a "typical" urban Catholic parish in the United States. Our presenter was a priest-sociologist with a sure grasp of the demographic data and a good pastoral sense. Based on

3. See Howard L. Dayton, Jr., *Your Money Counts: The Biblical Guide to Earning, Spending, Saving, Investing, Giving, and Getting Out of Debt* (Carol Stream, IL: Tyndale House Publishers, 1997).

census data and other studies, he commented on the circumstances and experiences that are likely to shape a contemporary congregation: stresses and strains on marriage and child raising, divorce rates, dating patterns, incidence of addiction to alcohol and narcotics, notions of authority and volunteerism, quality of religious education, influence of media, etc. It was an impressive list, laid out on a grid that appeared to touch every aspect of modern life. When the speaker opened the floor for discussion, however, one of the lay members of our board raised his hand and said, "One thing is missing from your list . . . *work!*" The awkward silence that followed was an eloquent commentary—how could one overlook something that commands people's time and shapes their attitudes and aspirations in such a profound way?

But silence about work and professional life—and all of the practical realities about money and management that go with it—is not uncommon in the pulpit and in the consciousness of many pastoral leaders. That little is said in the pulpit about the experience of working for a living is a consistent lament from laity. Preachers may feel they have little to say about one of the most defining experiences of their parishioners' lives. And parishioners may wonder if any significant connection can be made between their faith and their professional and work-a-day world.

And yet the financial and economic dimensions of institutional life ground us in reality like few other matters do. While the leaders of a religious institution may have a thoroughly noble mission and a beautiful vision of how they want to fulfill that mission, if they do not have the resources to sustain their work, little will be accomplished. The often-repeated slogan—"no margin, no mission"—has an inevitable truth about it. And here, perhaps more than in any other part of the responsibilities of an administrator, the need to be attentive to the common good, to keep in mind the welfare of the entire community, is paramount. A recent study of presidents of seminaries and theology schools conducted by the Auburn Center for Theological Education concluded that financial stewardship was the single most important factor in determining the success of a president's tenure.[4]

A prime responsibility of the administration of any institution—and in particular religious institutions who seldom suffer from an abundance of financial resources—is to maintain what some have called an "economic equilibrium."[5] An "economic equilibrium" means that an institution maintains enough financial resources to sustain its mission; that is, having enough resources to compensate its personnel with a just wage; being able to provide and sustain physical facilities needed to carry out its mission; providing the everyday resources (equipment, operating funds, etc.) for the members of the institution to do their vital work; and maintaining the purchasing power of the institution's assets (e.g., its endowment or financial reserves). Most religious institutions hope that their mission is important enough that they can do more than maintain "equilibrium" and want to expand and develop—for this, of course, even more financial resources will be needed. But on a basic level—given the economic status where in fact

4. Barbara G. Wheeler, G. Douglass Lewis, Sharon L. Miller, Anthony T. Ruger, David L. Tiede, *Leadership that Works: A Study of Theological School Presidents*, Auburn Studies 15 (December 2010).

5. See Anthony Ruger, John Canary, and Steven Land, "The President's Role in Financial Management," in *A Handbook for Seminary Presidents*, ed. C. Douglass Lewis and Lovett H. Weems Jr. (Grand Rapids, MI: Eerdmans, 2006), 90–91.

many religious institutions find themselves—even maintaining "economic equilibrium" is a bracing challenge.

Financial Management from a Biblical Perspective: The Meaning of Money

We might begin by asking ourselves, "What is the meaning of money in the first place?" What money means to us is one topic that receives relatively little consideration in theological circles. A few years ago, when I was asked to write on this topic from a biblical perspective, I could find few in-depth studies, particularly from Roman Catholic sources.[6] Evangelical authors have a much better track record in this area. Too often theological evaluations of money and its role in human experience can be confined to a prophetic evaluation of the dangers of wealth as a seduction of Christian values or as a symptom of inequity. Speaking too directly about acquiring money in some religious circles can seem a bit unseemly, and so is often referred to in euphemisms ("institutional advancement" or "development" or even perhaps, "stewardship"!). Vigilance about the misuse of money is, of course, a valid perspective rooted in the Gospel, but it does not exhaust the meaning of money in human experience or in Christian life.

Money has complex and diverse meanings in various cultures on both a personal and social level, but some fundamental meanings stand out in our Western culture. For example,

6. My own effort to tackle this subject can be found in "Financial Support for the Church and Our Biblical Heritage," *New Theology Review* 9 (1996): 38–51; some of the following reflections on money are adapted from an essay I prepared for a commentary included in *The Reluctant Steward Revisited*.

one way to think of money and other material possessions is to view them as *extensions of our person*. Some philosophers and theologians have reflected on the meaning of our bodies as extensions of our spirit or soul. In other words, body and spirit are not separable components that make up the human being, but the body is an expression of our spirit—we are embodied beings. We extend our body in outreach and embrace as we mature and develop in our relational capacity.

Furthering this view, we can think of our possessions, properly used, as extensions of our body. Our clothing, our homes and its furnishings, our computer and our automobile, and our financial resources themselves are means of extending our own physical and spiritual being into a wider sphere of communication and influence. Investment of money allows a person to project his or her influence into the future, and a bequest or trust allow donors to continue to have an impact on an institution, a cause, or a loved one even beyond their own lifetime. And just as financial resources can be viewed as an "extension" of an individual so, too, financial resources help an institution extend its reach to the wider public it is meant to serve.

Another function of money in our society is as a *means of gauging the value or significance of one's work*. The CEO of a major corporation will earn a staggering salary under the assumption that his or her leadership will insure the company's profitability. The craftsmanship and materials that go into a Lexus make it more expensive than a Ford Focus. A brain surgeon earns more than an orderly. Of course the amount of money attached to a particular type of work or product can reveal a false evaluation on the part of the marketplace. Are the huge amounts of money given sports figures or movie stars based on an accurate assessment of their worth to society, or are such salaries a symptom of distorted societal values? And factors other than money can signal the importance or value of one's work. The salary of the president of the United States is insignificant alongside some corporate and media salaries, but there are a lot of other perks and signs of prestige that clearly signal the importance society attaches to that office. It may seem counterintuitive but nevertheless is true that people are more likely to give to causes and institutions that are financially successful rather than to those in desperate financial need. A religious school or a charitable organization that is financially sound is viewed by many donors as one that is worth supporting.

Money can also give us *a sense of security*. We need to have enough money to put food on the table, a roof over our heads, to educate our children and so on. If we lose our job or make a bad investment, we face the specter of being out on the street. I remember my mother telling me that her father, an immigrant from Ireland, was constantly worried about losing his job and not having enough money to feed his family of seven daughters and one boy! That anxiety, she was convinced, shortened his life. Having adequate money can give us the needed security to face the rest of life's challenges. At the same time, we know that money can also create a false sense of security as well. Such was the message of Jesus' parable about the man who solves the problem of having too great a harvest. Instead of sharing his wealth, he builds more barns to hoard it—only to lose his life on that same day (see Luke 12:16-21). Having an abundance of money does not automatically give us ultimate security about the meaning of our lives.

One other important meaning attached to money in our society is its role as *a medium of exchange and a symbol of relationship*. "Exchange" is an important value in our economic culture and money is a medium of exchange. This is clear, of course, when we exchange money to purchase some goods or services. But there are also more subtle forms of exchange, as when we tip the waiter in the restaurant in exchange for good service. Or, in a more compromised example, when someone hoping to win a city contract slips an envelope of cash across a politician's desk. Lots of earnest Christians send donations to religious shrines or to television evangelists in the hope that some favor or cure might result.

Such "exchange" can take place even in the most altruistic and gracious circumstances, and here money can be symbolic of love and friendship and the medium of an authentic gift. The money tucked with love in the card given to a grandchild at their First Communion or graduation, or the donation given to a church or school as a sign of support and solidarity, expresses love and commitment. In these instances money becomes the medium through which the donor expresses his or her relationship to a treasured cause and, in return, those who give experience an affirmation of their own worth, feel the satisfaction of doing good, and are able to stand in solidarity with the people and causes they believe in. Money placed in the collection basket or given as a gift to a religious cause can also be an expression of pure gratitude to God—gratitude that can be an expression of the realization that all of life is a divine gift or, in many instances, an expression of gratitude for what appears to be an act of God's own love for us when health is restored or a troubling problem resolved.

These commonplace symbolic dimensions of money (which certainly do not exhaust its range of meaning) illustrate its importance in daily human experience. The use of money is closely connected with human productivity, self-expression, and self-worth, and it is interwoven with some of our deepest and most powerful relationships. Money enables us to extend our reach, for better or worse, and to express our love and appreciation and gratitude.

The Meaning of Giving

Recalling these meanings attached to money can also lead us into a proper theological assessment of what charitable giving means. The Bible itself has a fairly nuanced view of money and wealth, and it incorporates some of the symbolic dimensions mentioned above. Many strands of the Bible consider wealth as a sign of blessing from God, but the Scriptures also recognize that wealth can be acquired at the expense of the poor or deaden our attentiveness to the needs of others, as in Jesus' parable of the rich man and Lazarus (Luke 16:19-31). The lure of wealth could consume a person, claiming their ultimate allegiance—the famed "mammon of iniquity" mentioned by Jesus in the gospels (see Matt 6:24)—and deluding them into a false sense of security or self-sufficiency (as in the parable of the rich man and his barns in Luke 12:16-21). Jesus' stance of leaving behind the securities of home and resources is a prophetic challenge to such illusions. The "poor in spirit" recognize the ultimate truth of one's dependency on God for all life and every resource.

At the same time, the Scriptures do not demonize money and are filled with exhortations for those with resources, either goods or money, to share them with those in need. Ancient Israel itself had a fairly sophisticated and complex system of tithing to insure that the temple and its priesthood and the social and charitable institutions surrounding it were suitably financed. The giving of alms is one of the most important expressions of piety for both Israel and in the teachings of

Jesus. In the Sermon on the Mount, Jesus thoroughly endorses the giving of alms while warning against doing it for warped motives (see Matt 6:2-4). In these instances, money becomes a medium for expressing one's solidarity with a brother or sister. Descriptions of the ideal community of Jerusalem in Acts have the members sharing all things in common so that no one would be in need (Acts 2:44-45; 4:34-35), a reflection of the biblical vision for the covenant community of Israel.

Paul the apostle certainly appreciated both the practical and symbolic dimensions of money. In his First Letter to the Corinthians, Paul makes a vigorous defense of his right to financial compensation for his apostolic work when apparently some in the community had raised questions about it. "My defense against those who would pass judgment on me is this. Do we not have the right to eat and drink? Do we not have the right to take along a Christian wife, as do the rest of the apostles, and the brothers of the Lord, and Cephas? Or is it only myself and Barnabas who do not have the right not to work? Who ever serves as a soldier at his own expense? Who plants a vineyard without eating its produce? Or who shepherds a flock without using some of the milk from the flock?" (1 Cor 9:3-7). Despite defending his right to receive compensation, Paul in fact worked for a living so he could preach the Gospel "free of charge" (1 Cor 9:18).

Additionally, as we will note below, one of Paul's most elaborate pastoral initiatives was a massive collection for the "poor" of Jerusalem.[7] Paul knew the importance of "giving" as a Christian virtue. As any good preacher should do, when in doubt about his pastoral strategy, Paul decided to take up a collection! On behalf of the mother church of Jerusalem,

---

7. See below, pp. 125–30.

Paul organized an elaborate fund-raising campaign among the churches he had established in the Mediterranean world.

Paul's awareness of the practical and symbolic dimensions of money had a strong precedent in the texts and practices of Judaism. Money was one accepted medium of sacrifice to be offered to God in the Jerusalem temple, and practices such as tithing and the annual temple tax were key expressions of Jewish solidarity with each other and with God.

This all too brief reflection on some of the biblical notions of money and giving simply suggests that the meaning of money is complex and subtle. Money can be a sign of corruption or distorted priorities. But it can also be a means to extend one's power to do good to others and be expressive of the most gracious spiritual sentiments. I had many years of theological education under my belt before my ordination, but I do not recall ever hearing a discussion about the meaning of money. Yet money courses through our lives and that of our fellow Christians on a daily basis. To get beyond the diffidence many pastors and other religious leaders and administrators feel about asking for money will require that more thought be given to what money means to us as Christians in the first place.

As we have noted, hand in hand with understanding the meaning of money is understanding the meaning of giving. As Robert Lynn asked in his commentary on the original "Reluctant Steward" study, why should we give at all?[8] It is a question to be posed not only for potential donors but also for those whose responsibility may be to invite people to give.

8. Robert W. Lynn, "Faith and Money: The Need for a New Understanding of Stewardship," in *The Reluctant Steward*, ed. Daniel Conway, Anita Rook, and Daniel A. Schipp (Indianapolis, IN and St. Meinrad, IN: Christian Theological Seminary and St. Meinrad Seminary, 1992), 31.

When we recognize that one of the crucial meanings of money in our culture is self-expression and an extension of our own personal capacity, giving money to a cause or community is understood not only as a tax or a sacrifice but also as a sign of solidarity and commitment. This puts the spotlight on the worthiness of the cause and the trustworthiness of those who lead the community. It is an axiom of fund-raising that donors give to people and causes they trust. Recent studies of giving patterns confirm that confidence with how the Church manages its money and reassurance about what it is used for are critical for member satisfaction. From this perspective, giving money to a Christian community or institution that uses it well enables Christian donors to lead an authentic Christian life. They are giving of themselves for the sake of the other—the very heart of the Christian ethic.

Giving, then, is an expression of discipleship—one of the fundamental principles rightly affirmed in all stewardship programs. Conversely, reluctance or refusal to give can be a sign of an undeveloped Christian life, that is, the inability to transcend oneself for the sake of the other. But in some instances, a refusal or reluctance to give may be a practical judgment on the part of the Christian community about the trustworthiness of their church and its leaders. Thus money and giving are experiences deeply entwined with ordinary human experience. Practical economic realities are on the minds and hearts of good people every day of their lives.

Financial Administration as Christian Stewardship

"Stewardship" is an important biblical and theological concept in speaking of the administration of financial resources. In 1992 the National Conference of Catholic Bishops issued a pastoral letter entitled, "Stewardship: A Disciple's Response."[9] Although intended to boost charitable giving on the part of Catholics, the bishops took a broad approach to the topic, so much so that some critics felt the bishops were also reluctant to talk directly about money! But, in fact, the bishops wanted to lay the proper biblical and theological groundwork for the Christian use of financial resources before moving into the specific means of doing so. The bishops' statement defined a Christian steward as one "who receives God's gifts gratefully, cherishes and tends God's gifts responsibly, shares God's gifts in love and justice, and returns God's gifts with increase." Christian stewardship, in the perspective of the bishops, covered a broad spectrum of responsibility: to creation itself through respect for the environment, to the use of our gifts in our own God-given vocation in our family life and in our everyday work, to collaborating in the mission of the Church and supporting that mission.

As the bishops' statement illustrates, this notion of stewardship has a strong biblical basis. The Bible presents all of creation, including the creation of the human person, as a gift of God to be used responsibly and gratefully. When Israel is ultimately brought into the Promised Land, the Bible, particularly in the book of Deuteronomy, repeatedly makes clear that the land is a pure gift and has not been earned by Israel. The parents of Israel are told to remind their children: "We were once slaves of Pharaoh in Egypt, but the LORD brought us out of Egypt with his strong hand and wrought before our eyes signs and wonders, great and dire, against Egypt and against Pharaoh and his whole house. He brought us from there to lead us into

9. United States Conference of Catholic Bishops, *Stewardship: A Disciple's Response* (Washington, DC: USCCB, 1997).

the land he promised on oath to our fathers, and to give it to us. Therefore, the LORD commanded us to observe all these statues in fear of the LORD, our God, that we may always have as prosperous and happy a life as we have today; and our justice before the LORD, our God, is to consist in carefully observing all these commandments he has enjoined on us" (Deut 6:20-25).

The Bible urges the Israelites never to forget that they had been gifted by God and because they themselves were strangers adrift in a foreign land, they should never neglect the "widow, the orphan, and the sojourner" (see, for example, Deut 10:17-19). Thus as the bishops' statement notes, those faithful to God receive God's gifts gratefully, cherish and deal with those gifts responsibly, and share those gifts with others in love and justice.

This is clearly the teaching of Jesus in the New Testament. Steeped in the piety of his Jewish tradition, Jesus, through his parables and sayings, repeatedly called for generous use of one's resources on behalf of the poor and vulnerable. The rich young man who sought new life was encouraged to "sell [his possessions] and give to the poor" (Matt 19:21). And so, too, in Luke's "Sermon on the Plain," the disciples are told: "Do not be afraid any longer, little flock, for your Father is pleased to give you the kingdom. Sell your belongings and give alms" (Luke 12:32-33). In his parable, Jesus mocks the rich man who built new barns to store his abundant harvest and then commends himself for his own self-indulgence: "I shall say to myself, 'Now as for you, you have so many good things stored up for many years, rest, eat, drink, be merry!'" (Luke 12:19). That night this same man would face death! (Luke 12:20). Likewise, in the story of the rich man and Lazarus, the rich man steps over the starving and sick Lazarus who is lying at his doorstep and thus earns God's condemnation (Luke 16:19-31).

The Wise Use of Money

A number of Jesus' sayings deal with those who in fact give alms but do it for self-aggrandizement. Thus Jesus condemns the hypocrisy of those who "blow a trumpet" to advertise their generosity (Matt 6:2) and praises the widow who quietly gives all of her coins for the temple upkeep—a gift that exceeds in generosity the lavish gifts of the wealthy who give to draw notice to themselves (Mark 12:41-44). The Pharisee who stands at the front of the sanctuary and proclaims his own virtue—including paying tithing "on my whole income"—is contrasted with the sincerity of the tax collector who doesn't dare lift his eyes and beats his breast in repentance (Luke 18:9-14). On the other hand, Zacchaeus, a wealthy man and a tax collector, perched in his sycamore tree in order to get a glimpse of Jesus passing by, earns the honor of hosting Jesus through his pledge of giving half his possessions to the poor (Luke 19:1-10).

Jesus also warns that obsession with money can be a dangerous seduction: "No one can serve two masters. He will either hate one and love the other, or be devoted to one and despise the other. You cannot serve God and [money]" (Matt 6:24). The disciples are encouraged to leave their possessions behind in order to have the freedom to follow Jesus (for example, Mark 10:28-31)—a sacrifice the rich young man sadly cannot yet make (Matt 19:16-22). In John's Gospel, Judas's downfall in betraying Jesus seems to have begun in his misuse of the community purse (John 12:6).

Along with these warnings about the seduction of wealth are also teachings about the wise use of resources. In the parable of the talents, the servant who invests the master's resources and earns an increase is praised (Matt 25:14-30). When challenging would-be disciples to consider the cost,

Jesus speaks about the need for someone who is considering a building project to first estimate the cost! (Luke 14:28-30). Likewise, Jesus holds up the example of the wily steward who, when about to be fired, feathers his own nest at the expense of his master's resources by settling debts with potential future donors, a lesson that shows that "the children of this world are more prudent in dealing with their own generation than are the children of life" (Luke 16:1-8).

Exhortations about the wise use of financial resources are also found in other New Testament writings directed at the life of the early Church. The early chapters of the Acts of the Apostles portray the Jerusalem community as a fulfillment of the covenant ideals of Israel where the Israelites' care for each other would mirror God's own faithful care of Israel. So, too, in the first community of Christians, everyone held "all things in common," selling their property and possessions and divid[ing] them among all according to each one's need" (Acts 2:44-45). In this fervent early community, "There was no needy person among them, for those who owned property or houses would sell them, bring the proceeds of the sale, and put them at the feet of the apostles and they were distributed to each according to need" (Acts 4:34-35).

Along with these beautiful ideals of sharing all things in common, Luke also reminds us that this was a human community prone to failure, so the generous example of Barnabas who sells a piece of property and gives it to the community (4:36-37) is contrasted with the selfish deceit of Ananias and Sapphira who attempt to cheat the community, retaining for themselves some of the profits from the property they purport to sell on behalf of the community (5:1-11). Likewise, one of the first signs of dissension in the community is the complaint of the Greek-speaking Jewish Christians that their widows were being neglected compared with the widows of the Hebrew-speaking

Jewish Christians (Acts 6:1). This leads to the leaders (the administrators!) making an adjustment by appointing "deacons" to oversee the daily distribution of goods to those in need.

The Letter of James is another New Testament text that speaks forcefully about the judicious use of money and possessions. The leaders of the community are sternly warned not to show partiality to the wealthy at the expense of the poor, using an example that still rings true today. The rich benefactors are given prime seats in the assembly while the poor person in shabby clothing is shuttled to the back of the room! (Jas 2:1-13). Drawing on the tradition of the prophets and the teaching of Jesus himself, James condemns those who become absorbed in their wealth while "withholding wages from the workers who harvest your fields" (Jas 5:1-6).

Right use of finances and possessions, particularly on the part of community leaders, is a particular concern of the Pastoral Epistles, First and Second Timothy and Titus. Although attributed to Paul, these letters were probably written shortly after the death of the apostle at a time when the Christian community was becoming more concerned about its structures and organization. There are exhortations about the importance of authentic teaching and good conduct on the part of leaders mentioned throughout all three letters. But there is also a concern about the proper management of the community. Leaders of the community such as *episkopoi* or "overseers" should "not be . . . [lovers] of money" and should have demonstrated that they can manage their own household before being entrusted with management of the community's own resources (1 Tim 3:3-4). Likewise, "deacons" should "not [be] greedy for sordid gain" and also give evidence they can manage "their households well" (3:8, 12). Leaders of the community should also make sure that those members of the community "who toil in preaching and teaching" are paid a just wage

(5:17-18). Those who are consumed with the love of money will fail, "for the love of money is the root of all evils" (6:10).

Thus in both the teaching of Jesus—drawing on his Jewish heritage—and in the exhortations of the New Testament, leaders of the community are to be good stewards of the resources entrusted to them. As we learn today from the sad examples of leaders in business and politics as well as those who head charitable organizations, money can have a corrosive effect. Who does not wince when we hear of the leaders of supposedly philanthropic or religious organizations intended to serve the poor and the needs of society instead siphoning off precious resources to provide themselves with perks and the good life? And in a time when so many people are in desperate need of food and housing and other essentials for a decent life, we can only be outraged when learning of the staggering amount of waste in government and in other civic organizations because of poor management. Our biblical heritage gives us another vision of how money and resources are to be used. Those entrusted with leadership are to be good stewards of the resources entrusted to them on behalf of the community, recognizing that the resources they administer are ultimately a gift from God to be used in service for others, particularly for those most in need.

Fund-Raising

In today's world, few leaders of religious institutions are exempt from having to raise money to support their mission. Pastors not only have to ask for support from the pulpit from time to time but also are often expected to lead significant capital campaigns for facility repairs or new construction or to reduce the parish debt. At the very least, local leaders are expected to participate in diocesan-wide or regional capital campaigns. Presidents of religiously sponsored colleges and universities often spend a majority of their time and energy on fund-raising. The same is true of heads of charitable organizations, hospitals, and seminaries. Even institutions such as diocesan seminaries and other diocesan entities that formerly could count on being fully subsidized from diocesan funds must now themselves do direct fund-raising to supply or supplement the money that used to be given directly to them. Much of this fund-raising responsibility falls in the lap of the president or director of a religious institution or the pastor of the parish. But few successful fund-raisers are lone rangers. Instead they depend on the assistance of professionals who are part of their staff or on an army of volunteers who share the task of acquiring necessary support for an institution.

Fund-Raising as a Christian Vocation

Here again our goal in this discussion is not to offer advice on how fund-raising should be done but to reflect on how this aspect of institutional life is itself an expression of the Christian vocation. Few aspects of administrative work draw on all the dimensions of institutional life the way fund-raising does. The leader who musters financial support from the wider population for his or her institution must be fully committed to the mission of the institution and has to be able to articulate that mission in a convincing, even passionate, manner. The fund-raiser needs to have a capacity to connect with people in a respectful and warm manner and to build friendships for the institution. And they must project a genuine sense of integrity, helping to reassure prospective donors that their gifts will be used for the purpose intended and that management of the institution's finances is in good hands. At its heart, effective fund-raising is relational—building a wider community of care and commitment for an institution's life beyond the perimeter of its walls.

In his thoughtful book *The Spirituality of Fundraising*, the noted spiritual writer Henri Nouwen, puts his finger on a fundamental dimension of fund-raising seen from a Gospel perspective.[10] He notes at the outset: "Fundraising is a subject we seldom think about from a spiritual perspective. We may think of fund-raising as a necessary but unpleasant activity to support spiritual things. Or we might believe that fund-raising reflects a failure to plan well or to trust enough that God will provide for all our needs. Indeed, quite often fund-raising is a response to crisis."[11] Yet none of these perspectives are adequate from a Gospel perspective. Fund-raising, Nouwen insists, is integral to our discipleship. It is a matter of "proclaiming what we believe in such a way that we offer other people an opportunity to participate with us in our vision and mission." "We invite people to invest themselves in a great enterprise through the resources that God has given them: their energy, their prayers, their money."

Through our work of fund-raising, he notes, we are in fact collaborating with the Gospel call to conversion. In Greek the word *metanoite*, often translated as "convert" or "repent," literally means "to change our perspective," or to "change the way we see and understand things," deriving from the root word *nous* meaning mind and the prefix *meta* which implies change or transformation. Thus in the famous passage in Mark 1:14-15 where Jesus' sounds the keynote of his mission—"The time is at hand. The kingdom of God is at hand. Repent (*metanoite*) and believe in the gospel"—he is in fact summoning his disciples to "repent" or "convert" in the sense of a fundamental change in perspective; in effect, to see things in a new way, to grasp in a new way the mission of the coming kingdom of God and

10. Henri Nouwen, *A Spirituality of Fundraising* (Nashville TN: Upper Room Books, 2010).

11. Ibid., v–ix.

to commit to it. Inviting people to share in a mission that is part of bringing God's reign to our world is an opportunity for "conversion" or a fundamental "change in perspective." As Nouwen states, "If the cause is worthy, then we are helping people work to pave the way for God's kingdom. . . . The kingdom is where God provides for all that we need . . . and we become in a sense God's own voice inviting people to be part of making the reign of God come to fulfillment."

This, I think, is the heart of the matter. We cannot see the work of fund-raising on behalf of a worthy institutional mission as begging, or as a kind of Robin Hood operation of robbing the rich for the sake of the poor, or, as Nouwen says, to be motivated by resentment toward the rich for their good fortune or jealous of the opportunities they have. No, fund-raising from a Christian perspective is nothing less than collaboration in the work of building up the kingdom of God and of inviting our fellow Christians, our fellow human beings, to be engaged in something beautiful for God.

Paul as Fund-Raiser

One of the most important examples of fund-raising in the Bible is Paul's elaborate collection for the poor of Jerusalem. Paul decided to take up a collection in order to better connect the newly founded Christian communities in the wider Mediterranean world with the mother church in Jerusalem.[12] He asked each local community to take up a collection on

12. On Paul's references to the collection see Rom 15:25-30; 1 Cor 16:1-4; 2 Cor 8:1-24; 9:6-15; Gal 2:10. See further, Scot McKnight, "Collection for the Saints," in *Dictionary of Paul and His Letters*, ed. Gerald F. Hawthorne, Ralph P. Martin, and Daniel G. Reid (Downers Grove, IL: InterVarsity Press, 1993), 143–47.

"the first day of the week" (1 Cor 16:2) and then later Paul would combine the proceeds and, with representatives from each of the churches participating in the collection, bring the final sum to Jerusalem (this may have been the purpose of Paul's visit to Jerusalem mentioned in Romans 15:25-32 and Acts 24:14). Of special importance are the motivations Paul suggests to his Christians for contributing to the collection. Here we see fund-raising as an act of discipleship.

There are four reasons Paul gives for taking up his collection; reasoning found in his letters not in an organized way but culled from his various discussions of the project:

1. The first is most fundamental: to take care of the poor in Jerusalem. Significantly, Paul repeatedly calls the poor the "holy ones." For Paul, aiding the poor and the vulnerable was not just a matter of kindness or good human behavior, but it struck deep into his whole understanding of Christ and the God Jesus revealed. Paul knew from his own experience and from the deepest instincts of the Christian faith that the Jesus of the gospels identified with those who suffered and were the most vulnerable. "Whatever you do to the least of my brethren, you do to me."[13] According to the Acts of the Apostles, Paul had heard that profound message in his first encounter with the Risen Christ. "Saul" who was persecuting and imprisoning the Christians, including children and women, had a vision of the Risen Christ on the road to Damascus. "Saul, Saul why are you persecuting *me*?" (Acts 9:4-5). The Christ whom Paul encountered in his vision and the Christ he would proclaim

---

13. This quotation from the Last Judgment parable of the sheep and the goats found in Matthew 25:31-46 also forcefully proclaims this fundamental message: the Risen Christ identifies with those in need.

for the rest of his life was the Crucified and Risen Christ, a Christ especially present in those who suffered.

While in Dublin to give some lectures, I learned how Irish sign language expresses the name "Jesus Christ." Sign language, like all language, is not completely uniform but is shaped by the culture in which it is expressed. In the Irish "dialect" of sign language, the signer expresses the name Jesus Christ by indicating the nail marks in the hands of Jesus, pointing with his index finger at both sides of the hands. Thus Jesus Christ is identified through the wounds of his Crucifixion. Also in the resurrection accounts in the Gospels of Luke and John: The Risen Christ appears to the apostles with the wounds of his Crucifixion still apparent. And in one of the most dramatic scenes in all of the Gospel literature, Thomas is invited to touch those wounds in Jesus' hands and feet and side in order to experience that the Risen Jesus is also the Crucified Jesus. The deepest reality of our faith is that the compassion of God for those most vulnerable is revealed through a Crucified Jesus—the astounding assertion of Christian faith—that God is present and works in the world through the least, through what Paul called the "weak" (1 Cor 1:26-31). The life-giving abundance of the resurrection comes through the love that led Jesus to give his life for others.

This profound Christian conviction echoes the entire Bible's image of God and deepens it: God hears the cry of the poor. Here is a fundamental link between the use of our resources on behalf of the poor and the deepest wellsprings of our faith—the conviction realized by saints throughout our history. The face of the Crucified Christ is found on the face of those who suffer. What we do to them we do to Christ. Thus a collection on behalf of the poor becomes a profound act of Christian discipleship.

2. A second motivation for Paul was that the collection enabled the Gentile churches scattered throughout the Mediterranean world to express their solidarity with the Jewish-Christian Church of Jerusalem and thereby with each other. They all formed one body, the Body of Christ, the Crucified Body of Christ. So, as Paul told his community in Corinth, we are many members but one body and when one suffers we all suffer, when one is in need, we are all bereft (1 Cor 12:12-27). For Christians, those in need are not objects to be pitied but fellow members of the Body of Christ to be respected and honored.

This is an aspect of fund-raising and charitable giving that Pope Francis has strongly emphasized—what he calls "accompaniment." Inviting people with resources to share their gifts with those in need is also an invitation for them to experience the reality of other peoples' lives, to come into relationship with them. "The poor have much to teach us. Not only do they share in the *sensus fidei* [the Latin term for the "sense of the faith" held by the members of the Church], but in their difficulties they know the suffering Christ. We need to let ourselves be evangelized by them. The new evangelization is an invitation to acknowledge the saving power at work in their lives and to put them at the center of the Church's pilgrim way. We are called to find Christ in them, to lend our voice to their causes, but also to be their friends, to listen to them, to speak for them and to embrace the mysterious wisdom which God wishes to share with us through them" (EG 198).[14]

14. Excerpts of this translation are from Pope Francis, *Evangelii Gaudium* (The Joy of the Gospel) (Washington, DC: United States Conference of Catholic Bishops, 2013).

The pope continued, "Our commitment does not consist exclusively in activities or programs of promotion and assistance; what the Holy Spirit mobilizes is not an unruly activism, but above all an attentiveness which considers the other 'in a certain sense as one with ourselves.' This loving attentiveness is the beginning of a true concern for their person which inspires me effectively to seek their good. This entails appreciating the poor in their goodness, in their experience of life, in their culture, and in their ways of living the faith. True love is always contemplative, and permits us to serve the other not out of necessity or vanity, but rather because he or she is beautiful above and beyond mere appearances" (EG 199).

3. Paul also told his communities that their giving to those in need was a way of expressing gratitude to God for the gifts and opportunities they had received. As noted previously, one of the symbolic meanings of money is as an extension of ourselves—just as clothing and all our possessions are in a certain way extensions of ourselves.[15] We reach out and extend and express ourselves through the things we have. Sometimes our possessions get in the way of expressing our true selves and we are burdened and trapped by what we own. But we can and do use money—our resources—to express our love and gratitude to others. And, Paul reminded his Christians, this was a way of exchange, of expressing our love and gratitude to God by helping God's own children thrive. So here is another connection to the deepest values of our faith: generosity in our use of our resources—personal or corporate—can be an expression of gratitude to God from whom all good things come. To invite someone to express their gratitude to God for the gifts they themselves have been given in their lives by

15. See above, pp. 109–13.

giving to a worthy cause is also to invite them to be a grateful disciple of Christ.

4. And, finally, Paul motivates his fellow Christians to be generous because in contributing to the Jewish-Christian Church in Jerusalem, the Gentile churches were participating in the great act of reconciliation of the world, helping to heal the breach between Jew and Gentile, between rich and poor, between cultures and peoples and traditions. In the letter to the Romans, Paul saw the relationship between Israel and the Gentiles as the final drama of the world's salvation and he earnestly prayed that it would come soon. The collection was a visible, practical way to help build those bridges, to bring about reconciliation. Jewish tradition speaks about philanthropy or charity as helping to "heal or repair the world" (*tikun ha olam*). Paul speaks of that same concept in his letters, as do the Epistles to the Ephesians and Colossians—breaking down the dividing wall and making the two one (Eph 2:11-22). Right use of resources, from a Christian and biblical point of view, makes us collaborators with God in building up the world and bringing about the reconciliation of all things.

So, the work of fund-raising as explained by Paul touches a profound expression of our Christian faith: by recognizing the face of the Crucified and Risen Christ in the face of the poor and vulnerable, by encouraging our fellow Christians to give in a spirit of solidarity of faith and love as members of the one Body of Christ, by using our resources as an expression of profound thanksgiving to God for the gift of life, and by understanding that through our contributions to human thriving and to alleviating the burden of suffering and division we are privileged to share in God's own creative work of reconciling and redeeming our world.

"Staying Awake"

There is one other dimension of fund-raising that deserves mention. In Mark's Gospel, shortly before the beginning of his arrest and passion, Jesus exhorts his disciples to "stay awake" (Mark 13), that is, to be alert to the presence of grace and the coming of Christ breaking into the ordinary rhythms of everyday life. In his wonderful book *Life Together* (cited previously), the Lutheran theologian, pastor, and modern-day martyr, Dietrich Bonhoeffer emphasized the need for anyone who wanted to be part of an authentic Christian community to have a firm grip on reality. He wrote this brief and eloquent book as a rule of life for a clandestine seminary hidden from the watchful and hostile eyes of the Gestapo in the waning months of World War II. Its mission was to create a new generation of pastoral leaders who would be able to take a prophetic stance against the evils of National Socialism. In his chapter on "community," Bonhoeffer warns against "wish dreamers"—those who, as he says, are more in love with the ideal community of their own dreams than they are with the actual community that God gives them.

My own experience in fund-raising over many years—relating to donors, asking their help, being a part of their lives—was that it kept me "awake" about ordinary human experience that I might not be alert to simply within the confines of my life as a priest, a teacher, or scholar. Perhaps the same might be true in many other religious institutions. Fund-raising brings the fund-raiser into vital contact with everyday human beings in all of their reality. In effect, the fund-raiser mediates between the donors' circumstances and their hopes and dreams and the mission of the institution one serves. On the one hand, the fund-raiser has to be worldly wise about the importance of money and its significance for the donor. Jesus, we recall, praised "the children of this world [who] are more prudent in dealing with their own generation than are the children of light" (Luke 16:1-8). At the same time, the fund-raiser, articulating the mission of the institution he or she serves, can also bring awareness to donors about the experiences of the poor and vulnerable, the global scope of our Catholic and Christian experience, and the need for young people to be formed in the values and practices of our faith—realities that sometimes even very successful people can be shielded from. I vividly recall one of the first fund-raising activities I was involved in as president of CTU. One of our board members graciously held a reception in his home, inviting friends and neighbors to hear about the CTU story. I spoke for a few minutes, not really feeling so confident that I had been persuasive. When I finished I found myself standing next to one of the guests I did not know—as our host was saying a few words, the guest leaned over to me and said, "Father, don't underestimate how much people like us care about the Church and its future." I had presumed I would have to create concern about supporting the Church in my audience, but this man reminded me that lay members of the Church care a great deal about their spiritual home.

For the Catholic community, this was the clarion call of the Second Vatican Council's *Gaudium et Spes*, the famous pastoral constitution on the Church in the Modern World which began with these words: "The joy and hope, the grief and anguish of the [people] of our time, especially of those who are poor or afflicted in any way, are the joy and hope, the grief and anguish of the followers of Christ as well. Nothing that is genuinely human fails to find an echo in their hearts. For theirs is a community composed of [people], of [people] who, united in Christ and guided by the holy Spirit, press onwards towards the kingdom of the Father and are bearers of a message of salvation intended for all [people]" (GS 1).[16]

Conclusion

Therefore, fund-raising on behalf of the kingdom of God is a noble Christian profession, a true Christian ministry—one with deep roots in our biblical history, in the mission of Jesus and the early Church. As Nouwen affirmed, fund-raising is nothing less than a vital expression of authentic discipleship, enabling the daughters and sons of God to participate in Jesus' mission of healing and transforming our world.

Thus from the viewpoint of our Christian heritage, finances and fund-raising are not alien activities or purely secular tasks that have to be endured but are capable of being true expressions of our vocation as disciples of Jesus Christ.

16. Translation of Vatican II documents is from *Vatican Council II: The Conciliar and Postconciliar Documents*, trans. Austin Flannery (Collegeville MN: Liturgical Press, 2014).

6

Habits of the Heart

Every institution periodically faces the task of having to search for a new employee or staff member. Inevitably the supervisor involved has to draw up a "job description" that includes not only a list of the responsibilities of the position but also the personal and professional qualities sought in potential candidates.

Such job descriptions are a literary form all their own. While the list of duties is usually specific to the position involved, the desired personal qualities often reach for the ideal. The candidate for this position must be experienced, intelligent, competent, affable, collegial, trustworthy, honest, energetic, committed, and so on. After reading through such job descriptions, more than one wag has commented that Jesus himself might not be up to the job!

Yet at the same time, everyone realizes that a good administrator, especially one who is part of a religious institution, needs to have certain fundamental qualities. Without the proper motivation and necessary fundamental skills and qualities, someone taking a position in an institution whose purpose is ultimately to build up the kingdom of God will be a liability and not an asset. The candidate for the job has to "fit" into the spirit and values that permeate the institution and define its "culture." And it is also true that for someone working in an institution which has a noble purpose, the experience of striving to serve its mission in a thoughtful and responsible manner will enable that person to be a better human being and a more genuine Christian disciple.

So what are some of the "habits of the heart" or the spiritual qualities needed to serve well and with joy and satisfaction in the kinds of religious institutions we have been considering? And, conversely, what are the pitfalls that often face someone immersed in the work of administration? What, in effect, are the symptoms of a healthy institutional "spirituality" and what are some vital signs to be alert to?

Fortunately, two such lists—by two very different authors—come to mind. One is the helpful list described by Ann Garrido who, in her well-received book *Redeeming Administration*, identifies twelve "spiritual habits for Catholic leaders."[1] Garrido draws on her experience as a program director at the Aquinas Institute, a graduate school of theology in St. Louis, Missouri, to describe those spiritual qualities necessary for one to survive and, indeed, thrive as a human being and a follower of Christ in administrative service. Examples she adds from the lives of saints further define and exemplify these virtues.

The other list is the remarkable catalogue of fifteen "maladies" that Pope Francis presented to a startled group of cardinals, bishops, and other clerical officials of the Roman Curia on December 23, 2014. The day before, the pope had addressed the lay staff of Vatican City and had gone out of his way to praise them for their work and to thank them for their generous service. But at the traditional Christmas address to the Curia, the pope spoke bluntly about the spiritual ills that

1. See above, pp. xviii–xix.

can befall even those who serve at the highest levels of the Church's administration.

Both lists offer a good survey of the "habits of the heart" that administrators within a Christian institution should either foster or avoid. Many of these virtues and vices have already been implicit earlier in discussing the essential functions of administration: leadership, awareness of mission, prudent planning, building community, responsible use of resources, and so on. But these two lists underscore the kind of virtues and vices that are involved in administrative service, especially when viewed from the perspective of Christian life.

Good Spiritual Habits for Administrative Service

We turn first to virtues or "habits of the heart" that are necessary for effective administrative service and also likely to be fostered in one who serves in administration as an expression of their Christian vocation.[2]

1. The first "good spiritual habit" cited by Ann Garrido is that of "Breadth of Vision." Good leadership within any institution requires the leader have a sense of the "whole." In fact, the responsibilities of leadership pull one in that direction. In an academic institution, for example, faculty and some staff can do their jobs well by concentrating on their specific role within their classroom or office. Or in a parish, the leader of a particular group may believe that the life of the parish should

2. I should note at the outset that the descriptions of the twelve spiritual habits listed by Garrido are my own particular interpretation and illustration of her thoughts. While very grateful for this insightful list, I, rather than she, should be held accountable for them! They may or may not be described in the way that the original author intended.

revolve solely around their activities. But those in administrative leadership—whether the president of a school or the pastor of a parish—have to keep in mind and in balance the needs of the entire institution. As a president of a school of theology, I often felt the need for this wider perspective. A faculty member or someone on the staff might bring forward an idea or suggestion that had merit in itself, but I realized it would clash or not fit because of other circumstances in the institution of which the faculty or staff member were simply not aware.

As one commentator on good administrative leadership put it, the administrator cannot be content only to enjoy a dance with others in the ballroom but, from time to time, has to go to the balcony and view the patterns across the entire dance floor.[3] This necessary function of effective administrative leadership, Garrido observes, crosses over into a genuine Christian virtue when this view of the whole and care for the common good lead to "a wideness of spirit," a sense of "magnanimity" that ultimately reflects God's own "grand vision and spirit, leading one to experience something of how God sees and loves our universe"—a vision expressed in God's creation of the world described in Genesis and in God's enduring love for the world proclaimed by the entire Bible.

2. The second virtue both required by and fostered by administrative experience is that of "generativity." To be an effective administrator, one is compelled to go beyond the "status quo" and try things that are new or different. I remember as a beginning faculty member suggesting some possible new

3. See Ronald A. Heifetz and Marty Linsky, *Leadership on the Line: Staying Alive through the Dangers of Leading* (Cambridge, MA: Harvard Business School Press, 2002).

projects to my supervisor. I found that whenever I made suggestions like this that the supervisor unconsciously sighed out loud and would then remind me of all the projects that had piled up on his desk. I soon got the picture that my suggestions (which may well have been naive or impractical) were not particularly welcome! If an administrator's office becomes a place where good ideas come to die and where things remain static, then that sector of the institution will soon atrophy. Bringing one's energy and enthusiasm—that is, one's "generativity"—to administrative work, in fact, reflects the dignity and beauty of work that God has entrusted to us as stewards of creation and is thus a genuine opportunity for virtue.

3. The third spiritual habit is that of "trust." The "trust" Garrido has in mind has several dimensions. First of all is trust of others. Some administrators are convinced that only they have the insight and energy to accomplish a particular task in the right way and thus are wary of entrusting it to others. But, over time, the thoughtful—and humble—administrator learns to trust others and realize that their colleagues, too, are committed to their work and capable of getting things done.

Another level of trust is trust in ourselves. Many people with responsibilities in an organization fear failure or feel very inadequate for the many tasks they are expected to do. Here, too, time and common sense can help us be more serene and accept both our strengths and our weaknesses as human beings. And, finally, there is the need for trust in the value of our work and that of the institution we serve. Does it really make any difference? Will the world be a better place because of what I do? All of these expressions of trust ultimately rest in one's faith—and "trust"—in God's loving providence.

4. A fourth spiritual habit is that of "agape." Here Garrido draws on her theological background to define a type of love

that differs from "friendship love" and "romantic love" in that it has little to do with feelings. The Greek term *agape* refers to what can be described as "disinterested love," which is the kind of love that does not seek one's own self-interest but is "a commitment to the best interest of the other, even if one receives little or nothing in return." Classical spiritual writers were referring to this kind of love when they spoke of the virtue of "detachment." As noted above, "detachment" in this context does not mean indifference or a lack of engagement.[4] Rather it means learning to purify our love and service from the snares of our own personal needs. This kind of self-transcending love reflects the most profound of Christian virtues and is a form of love that those in administration have the opportunity to exercise. Often those in administration do not have the experience of knowing the full impact of their work. Unlike teachers who have the satisfaction of working with their students, physicians or nurses who personally encounter their patients, or counselors who can see improvement in their clients, administrators must often love "at a distance" and not directly see the impact of their work, thereby experiencing an authentic form of Christian love that does not expect anything in return. In fact, the gospels portray Jesus as animated by just such love: "The Son of man did not come to be served but to serve and to give his life as a ransom for many" (Mark 10:45).

5. "Integrity" is the fifth spiritual habit on the list. Often administrative responsibility involves directing others to do things in a proper way and with the proper spirit. As Garrido notes, this too can lead to greater integrity on our part: "There is nothing like being responsible for the execution of policies to make one start following them. When we are charged with

4. See above, pp. 99–101.

challenging others to live healthy, wholesome lives at the service of the common good, we will be immediately confronted with all those ways that we are not as healthy, wholesome, or cooperative as we should be." Aligning one's heart and spirit with our words and actions was a central teaching of Jesus and a source of conflict with his opponents. As Jesus told his disciples concerning his religious opponents, "Do and observe all things whatsoever they tell you, but do not follow their example. For they preach but they do not practice. They tie up heavy burdens hard to carry and lay them on people's shoulders, but they will not lift a finger to move them" (Matt 23:3-5). Thus, here is another example where administration carried out with integrity becomes an expression of Christian discipleship.

6. The sixth spiritual habit on the list is "humility." Administrators often have the chance—not always welcome for sure—to practice humility. Garrido cites some familiar examples: being asked in a meeting a question we cannot answer, losing our temper in public, missing a deadline, failing in an important project, and so on. Rather than attempting to avoid the truth by being defensive or fooling ourselves into thinking we are never wrong, such everyday humiliations can help us gain "a more accurate, truthful picture of ourselves" and, ultimately, learn to be comfortable with our own humanness. This is precisely what the Christian tradition names as "humility"—it is not a matter of dwelling on our weaknesses or becoming discouraged by our shortcomings, but, rather, being honest about who we are and being open to God's redeeming grace to help us grow as human beings and children of God. Paul the apostle understood the importance of such humility. Throughout his Christian life he was acutely embarrassed by the fact that he had once persecuted the Church of God

(see his lament in Gal 1:13 and Phil 3:6). But that did not dim his sense of vocation; he realized that he was weak and prone to failure but, at the same time, "we hold this treasure in earthen vessels, that the surpassing power may be of God and not from us" (2 Cor 4:7).

7. Seventh on the list is "courage." The virtue of humility, Garrido notes, has to find its complement in the virtue of courage. Those in administration, particularly at a leadership level, will often find themselves in difficult and unwelcome situations: confronting an errant colleague; having to make a difficult and perhaps unpopular decision; being thrust into a conflict one did not choose. Many times this involves dealing with personnel, including the most painful decision of having to let someone go. As Garrido accurately notes, many times such problem situations are connected to the symbolic dimensions of the roles that those in authority bear. Some people react instinctively in a negative way to those in authority, no matter who they are or what they do.

Threatening circumstances like these can lead administrators to plunge deep within their souls and to count on God's grace—the true source of Christian courage. Jesus had encouraged his disciples as they were sent out on mission, "Do not worry about how you are to speak or what you are to say. You will be given at that moment what you are to say. For it will not be you who speak but the Spirit of your Father speaking through you" (Matt 10:19-20). Similarly, Paul said to his disciple Timothy, "I remind you to stir into flame the gift of God that you have through the imposition of my hands. For God did not give us a spirit of cowardice but rather of power and love and self-control" (2 Tim 1:6-7). Many times in my own experience as an administrator I had to steel myself before walking into a difficult meeting or lifting the phone for a difficult call, and ask that God would be with me and help me find the right words to say.

8. Another key spiritual habit is that of "reflection." As Garrido points out, assessment and evaluation are important ingredients for effective administration. Administrators in today's world are constantly being asked to evaluate performance and achievement on the basis of empirical data. While others in an organization might be free to dream without constraint, administrators have to be aware of what actually worked and why. Tucked within this sometimes tedious aspect of administration is a genuine Christian habit of the heart—namely, the discipline of reflecting honestly and deeply on who we are and what we are doing with our lives. Traditionally, this type of reflection was called an "examination of conscience" or a "review of life." Coupled with a spirit of prayer and a trust in God's mercy, such reflection can help us know ourselves better and help us deepen our Christian life. The Jesus of the gospels often called his disciples to "come apart" for a while and pray, just as Jesus himself did (see, for example, Mark 6:30-32). Away from the din of the crowds and armed with a spirit of reflection, the Christian can renew his or her spirit and face the future with greater insight and courage.

9. Having a sense of humor, too, is a vital spiritual habit for those in administration. Being involved in the life of any institution can plunge us into situations that seem bizarre or absurd. Having a healthy sense of humor can help us cope with the sheer humanness of ourselves and the people with whom we serve. Garrido observes that some forms of humor border on the cynical and can mask a deep-seated anger or resentment. Or we might use humor to subtly denigrate someone else. Likewise, self-deprecating humor can be healthy and protect us from being too serious about ourselves, but, in

some instances, such humor can go too far and be a form of defensiveness or lack of confidence on our part.

What might be called "holy humor" draws attention to the absurdities of life but in such a way that it draws people to "laugh with" rather than "laugh at" others and their foibles. Garrido suggests that the humor implicit in many of Jesus' own teaching reflects this kind of humor: speaking, for example, of putting a light under a bushel basket, or taking the plank out of one's eye, or his parables praising clever rogues like the manager who fixes his accounts before being fired or the proud Pharisee who informs God of his many virtues. The Christian administrator is one who can laugh at the absurdities of life without, at the same time, losing an appreciation for the beauty and goodness of the world in which we live and work.

10. Surely one vital spiritual habit for administrators is a sense of "forgiveness." Anyone who has been involved in the life of an institution—no matter how enlightened and efficient it may be—will discover many occasions where forgiveness is called for. A sharp word from a supervisor or colleague; a lack of appreciation on the part of the leadership about the hard work of the staff; the drone of constant criticism on the part of some against those with authority; cold water dashed by a colleague on a treasured idea or suggestion—the list can be long. What might seem trivial slights to some become for others festering wounds hard to heal.

As Garrido and many others have pointed out, forgiveness is not the same as "forgetting." The old refrain, "forgive and forget" might work in some circumstances but not in most. The injury we have endured or injustice we experience is real and cannot simply be repressed as if nothing happened. The important thing is not forgetting an offense but how we respond after we have absorbed the blow. Rather than pretend nothing happened or submerging it for another day, forgiving someone is a profound Christian virtue, itself a gift of God. In the famous parable of the unforgiving servant in Matthew's Gospel, the wretch who is forgiven an enormous debt by his master—10,000 talents, the equivalent of the national gross product!—turns around and throttles a fellow servant who owes him only a small amount (Matt 18:21-35). The unforgiving servant's sin is forgetting that he himself had been given lavish forgiveness by his master. "Forgiving . . . from the heart," as Jesus entreats his disciples to do, comes from realizing who we are before God—that we, too, are prone to failure and to committing offense to others and, therefore, we should be compassionate and forgiving as God is to us.

Forgiveness in the workplace, as Garrido points out, might not mean immediate resolution of the cause of offense. Colleagues who have clashed may have to be content at first simply with avoiding further offense, pledging a recommitment to the mission of the institution, and working together in mutual respect, before they can build a close and warm bond of friendship.

11. The eleventh spiritual habit on Garrido's list may seem strange at first sight—namely, the virtue of "embracing death." What she is referring to is not dramatic martyrdom but the experience that most administrators have of many small everyday "deaths." The disappointment of failed plans, the loss of a trusted colleague who decides to move on for another opportunity, the slow pace of improvement and change, the misconstrual of one's motivations—all of these can become small "deaths" for our hopes, our dreams, our own self-understanding. I knew an experienced president of a school of theology who spoke of the "accumulation of small hurts" that had developed over the lifetime of his years of service.

One of the fundamental lessons I learned in many years of administrative service is that institutions have a life of their own—and no single person has absolute control of the institution's pace and direction. Despite the urgency one might feel about a project or initiative, the institution will move—or not move—in its own good time. These kinds of "deaths" or sufferings are not more noble or acute than those that come to human beings in many other circumstances. But in all these circumstances, Christians are asked to ultimately view such setbacks or sufferings not with a sense of despair or bitterness but to see them in the light of the death and resurrection of Jesus Christ. The deepest wellsprings of our faith invite us to view death not as the final word; life, not death, is the Christian destiny. Having that conviction deep within our soul can lead us to refuse to see even small "deaths" as overwhelming. Because of our faith in the Paschal Mystery, we can put in perspective the setbacks and failures in the world of the institution we serve and not be crushed by them but, instead, work through them to find new life.

12. Hope is the final spiritual habit on the list. As Garrido suggests, Christian hope is probably the virtue that gives meaning to everything else on the list. Christian hope is rooted in our faith in Christ's victory over death. The ultimate destiny of humanity from the perspective of Christian faith is not the cold and silence of death but vibrant and abundant life—life with God.

That same spirit of hope sustains effective administrators of any institution that sees itself as helping build up the kingdom of God. As Garrido notes, "Whether nonprofit or for profit, ecclesial or secular, the reason why any institution exists—if it is a healthy institution—is the belief that the world could be a better place than it is, and that through harnessing the member's efforts as a group, that institution can help make it so. In fits and starts, dribs and drabs, we limp along together with that dream ever before us." Every once in a while—especially at a time of setback—administrators need to recall the Emmaus story. In it, two disciples, discouraged by the death of Jesus and the apparent failure of their dreams ("we had hopes . . ."), encounter the Risen Christ and in his words and in the breaking of the bread have their hearts set on fire once again (see Luke 24:13-35). For someone who sees their role as an administrator as an expression of their vocation to discipleship, living in a spirit of hope is what sustains our commitment over the long haul. Dr. Craig Dykstra, former vice president of the Lilly Endowment and a wise Christian leader, spoke of religious institutions needing to commit to "long obedience in the same direction." In other words, institutions are called to persevere in commitment to their mission, a mission rooted ultimately in the quest for the kingdom of God.

Examining Our Consciences as Administrators of the Body of Christ

Two days before Christmas 2014, Pope Francis addressed the traditional gathering of the members of the Roman Curia.[5] He reminded his colleagues entrusted with the administration of the Church at its highest level that it was salutary to prepare for the feast of Christmas and the prospect of a New Year with an "examination of conscience." Viewed in the light of faith, those entrusted with the administration of the Church, the pope noted, are called to improve themselves

---

5. The full text, "Presentation of the Christmas Greetings to the Roman Curia. Address of his Holiness Pope Francis, Monday December 22, 2014," can be found on the Vatican website, https://w2.vatican .va/content/francesco/en/speeches/2014/december/documents/papa -francesco_20141222_curia-romana.html.

and "to grow in communion, holiness, and wisdom to realize its mission fully." In that light, he invited the cardinals, bishops, and other clerical members of the Curia involved in the Vatican's administration to be aware of the kind of "illnesses" (he used the Italian word for "maladies") and "temptations" that "weaken our service to the Lord."

Reading through the pope's remarkably colorful and blunt "catalogue of illnesses," I was struck how much they could serve as instruction not only for the members of the Roman Curia but also for anyone who desires to see their administrative service as, in fact, Christian service. Virtually everything on the pope's list describes obstacles and temptations facing anyone who is called to be an administrator at whatever level within an institution. Pope Francis's purpose—and the reason his list is included here—was not to discourage his colleagues but to support a healthy self-awareness and to be open to healing whatever professional illnesses we might have as those who exercise the gift of administration. Along with each "illness" described are also the pope's suggestions about the ways to offset and heal such administrative maladies.

The pope lists fifteen "maladies," most of which can be quickly defined:

1. First of all is what he calls **"the sickness of feeling oneself 'immortal,' 'immune,' or in fact 'indispensable.'"** This is the kind of attitude which characterizes those who "feel themselves superior to all and not at the service of all"—who "do not see the image of God imprinted on the face of others, especially the weakest and neediest." The remedy for this ill, the pope suggests, "is the grace to see ourselves as sinners and to say with all our heart: 'We are unworthy servants; we have only done what was our duty'" (Luke 17:10).

2. The second is the **"sickness of 'Martha-ism' . . . of excessive busyness"**—alluding of course to the Martha of

Luke's Gospel who was overly anxious about domestic tasks and received a gentle rebuke from Jesus (see Luke 10:38-42). To be overly immersed in our work to the neglect of necessary rest leads, the pope notes, "to stress and agitation." That is why Jesus himself called his disciples to "rest a while" (Mark 6:31).

3. The third is the sickness of **"mental and spiritual 'petrification.'"** This, the pope declares, describes those who have a "heart of stone" and "hide themselves under papers" while losing "the necessary human sensibility to make us weep with those who weep and rejoice with those who rejoice." This kind of hard-heartedness makes us lose the spirit of Jesus; whereas to be Christian means "to have the same sentiments that were in Christ Jesus, sentiments of humility and of self-giving, of detachment and generosity."

4. The fourth is the **"sickness of excessive planning and functionalism."** Here the pope apparently refers to those who become immersed in details and become like "an accountant or businessman" and settle down "in one's own static and unchanging positions." Surely the pope didn't mean to accuse all accountants and those in business of being "static" or "unchanging"; that can happen with any administrative position. The antidote is to be faithful to the Spirit who brings a sense of "freshness, imagination, and novelty" to our work.

5. The next on the list is **"the sickness of bad coordination."** A lack of communication with our colleagues can lead to a failure to collaborate. The pope cites in this regard Paul's reflections on the Body of Christ where the "foot says to the arm: 'I have no need of you,' or the hand to the head: 'I command,'" thus causing harm and scandal.[6]

---

6. The pope presents his own version of the body's soliloquy first presented by Paul. Instead of the foot speaking to the arm and the hand to the head,

6. The pope uses a particularly vivid metaphor in speaking of **"the sickness of spiritual Alzheimer's disease."** He refers here to those who forget "one's personal history with the Lord, forgetful of one's 'first love.'" This is the case of those who over time allow themselves to become oblivious to the ultimate purpose of their administrative service as an expression of their love for Christ and Christ's people.

7. The seventh malady on the list is the **"sickness of rivalry and vainglory."** He again turns to the admonitions of Paul who reminded the community in Philippi, "Do nothing out of selfishness or out of vainglory; rather, humbly regard others as more important than yourselves, each looking out not for his own interests, but [also] everyone for those of others." (Phil 2:1-4). Although not cited by the pope, Paul also wrestled with the corrosive impact of factions and rivalries within his communities (see, for example, Paul's concern about factions expressed in the opening paragraphs of his first letter to the Corinthians 1:10-17), a reality that also can create division and bitterness in any institution.

8. The pope turns to another strong medical metaphor in listing the **"sickness of existential schizophrenia."** He refers here to those who lead a "double life," addressing in a particular way clerics or religious who abandon any pastoral service and become immersed in bureaucratic affairs and end up living "a hidden and often dissolute life."

9. Next is the **"sickness of gossip, of grumbling, and of tittle-tattle."** He refers here to a malady that can take the life out of any organization, namely, those who become "sowers of discord" and manage to harm the reputation of their co-

---

Paul refers to the "eye" speaking to the "hand" and the "head" to the "feet." See Paul's entire metaphor of the Church as the Body of Christ in 1 Cor 12:12-31.

workers. This is a sickness of those, the pope notes, who, not having the courage to speak directly, speak behind one's back. Having worked in administrative service for many years, I realize that this type of "sickness" is a perennial problem, even among the most high-minded people and organizations. For a while at our institution, we were plagued by a staff member who seemed to make it her personal mission to go around spreading tales of woe—almost all of them fictitious. One of our staff told me that she used to close her office door when she heard this person making her way down the corridor!

10. The tenth is the **"sickness of divinizing directors."** By "divinizing" the pope refers to those employees who "court their superiors, hoping to obtain their benevolence." Or, conversely, of superiors who "court some of their collaborators to obtain their submission, loyalty, and psychological dependence." The pope is speaking bluntly here of one of the most toxic factors in an institution where the person in charge has "favorites" whom he or she rewards or where an employee is seen as manipulative in order to gain favor and advancement with a supervisor. The pope appeals to the strong words of Jesus condemning the religious leaders who act hypocritically and "do all their deeds to be seen by others" (Matt 23:8-12).

11. The sickness **"of indifference to others"** is next on the list. The pope's description of the symptoms of this illness is right to the point. This sickness manifests itself "when one thinks only of oneself and loses the sincerity and warmth of human relations." This type of person does not share his expertise with his fellow workers, hangs on to information that would help others, and, out of jealousy or cunning, takes joy in the failure of others, "instead of lifting him up again and encouraging him." Here, again, anyone who has served in an institution knows only too well this type of corrosive behavior.

12. The next illness is a characteristic target of Pope Francis, namely, **"the sickness of the mournful face."** In his beautiful exhortation *Evangelii Gaudium* (The Joy of the Gospel), the pope had challenged priests and religious who go around "look(ing) like someone who has just come back from a funeral" (EG 10). He levels the same challenge here to those who serve in an administrative capacity within the Church. Some can become "brusque and sullen," especially in dealing with subordinates. This type of behavior, the pope notes, is often symptomatic of "fear and one's own insecurity." The true follower of Jesus must learn "to be a courteous, serene, enthusiastic, and joyful person who transmits joy where he is." Anyone who works in a religious institution could name this kind of person whose bright spirit brings joy and encouragement to an organization.

13. The next malady might be specific to religious or priests within an organization—namely, the **"sickness of accumulating"**—but probably is good advice for everyone. This sickness affects people who accumulate an abundance of material possessions "not out of necessity but only to feel secure." Jesus' repeated exhortations to his disciples calls on them to "leave behind" whatever possessions stand in the way of their freedom to follow the call of the Gospel (Mark 10:28-31).

14. The **"sickness of closed circles"** is similar to that of the seventh on the list, that of "rivalry and vainglory." Here the pope refers to those who form their "little group" which over time becomes more important to them than belonging to the one Body of Christ! Often such closed circles cause great pain to others and create divisions and strife in the work environment of an institution.

15. The final sickness on the list is that **"of worldly profit, of exhibitionism."** This is the sickness that can overcome

an individual or a group that begins to operate more out of a love of power and seeking "worldly profits" while losing sight of their mission of serving God's reign on earth. This sickness is fundamental and is similar in a way to what the pope had described as "spiritual Alzheimer's" or "existential schizophrenia"—all maladies that cause the person working in the administration of a religious organization to forget the very purpose of their call to serve.

The pope concluded this remarkable "examination of conscience" by observing that these sorts of "sicknesses" were a danger not only to the Roman Curia but also to "every community, congregation, parish, and ecclesial movement" and "can strike at the individual as much as at the communal level." Healing of such illnesses is the work of the Holy Spirit and can happen when we become aware of the sickness and, through the power of the Spirit, make a "personal and communal decision to be cured, enduring the cure patiently and with perseverance."

Both the list of virtues proposed by Ann Garrido and the list of administrative "illnesses" presented by Pope Francis are deeply rooted in experience. Whoever has worked in a religious institution or organization, from the level of the parish and the school to the diocesan chancery or the Roman Curia, will recognize both the virtues and vices cited here. It is in this existential mix of virtue and vice, in these habits of the heart, that a genuine spirituality of administrative service can be found. Many of the strengths and failures found on these lists are true for the life and health of any organization. But from the point of view of the Gospel, the illnesses to be healed and the virtues to be cultivated form the very heart of what it means to be a follower of Jesus and to carry out one's discipleship in administrative service.

Conclusion

"Remembering Whose We Are"

Some years ago I came across a book that I found particularly helpful. It is titled *Forgetting Whose We Are*. Its subtitle reveals its special focus: *Alzheimer's Disease and the Love of God*.[1] It was written by David Keck, a missionary and biblical scholar whose own mother had been stricken by this disease at a relatively early age. His intent in writing this book was to try to understand this frightening disease in the light of the Gospel. He noted that Alzheimer's is particularly disturbing for a culture that emphasizes self-awareness and self-direction, a culture where we like to believe we are autonomous individuals and can do things "our way."

But, in fact, Keck notes, the experience of Alzheimer's challenges these values in a fundamental way. We are not as autonomous as we think we are—we come into this world and will leave this world dependent on the assistance of others. Nor are we really in control of our lives even when we might convince ourselves that we are. Above all, Keck notes, our memories are fragile, even if we are not afflicted by dementia or Alzheimer's. We often forget things and even what we

---

1. David Keck, *Forgetting Whose We Are: Alzheimer's Disease and the Love of God* (Nashville, TN: Abingdon, 1996).

think we remember may not be accurate. There is a whole legal industry that takes "depositions" from witnesses who have observed or experienced the same incident but whose memories of the event differ. We have come to learn about "repressed memories" and "distorted memories" and "false memories."

Keck transposes this set of human experiences about autonomy and memory to our Christian experience. Here, too, we have a hard time remembering not only who we are but also "whose" we are—that, in fact, we ultimately belong to God. As Christians, we use a whole set of "devices" to help us remember: the Scriptures themselves are, from one point of view, an effort to remember who we are, where we came from, and to whom we belong. So, too, are the liturgies we celebrate—recalling the great works of God that made us a people and that have saved us from our sin.

A key figure in the experience of coping with Alzheimer's is the "caregiver" who might be a family member or a professional health-care worker. When the persons who suffer from Alzheimer's can no longer remember their own name or that of their loved ones, when their own personal histories are no longer remembered by them, and when they are not even able to groom and care for themselves, their caregiver does not forget. The caregiver remembers the patient's name, their personal history, and their family network and continues to care for and groom the person with love and concern.

The "caregiver," in fact, is an image of the minister of the Gospel. People everywhere—even those who are fully healthy—can be prone to forget who they truly are and forget to whom they ultimately belong. For the sake of these, the Christian is called to serve as a "caregiver" to the world: dealing with others with respect, caring for them, and lovingly reminding them of the truth of their ultimate identity.

Keck ends his reflections on a strikingly beautiful note. Even if all forget, if the "caregivers" of humanity themselves were to forget, the Scriptures present God as the one who never forgets. Keck cites the beautiful text of Isaiah 49:

> But Zion said, "The LORD has forsaken me; my LORD has forgotten me." Can a mother forget her infant, be without tenderness for the child of her womb? Even should she forget, I will never forget you. See, upon the palms of my hands I have written your name." (Isa 49:14-16)

I found Keck's reflections helpful not only for coping with the experience of Alzheimer's disease (at the time I first read the book my own mother was suffering from this disease) but also in helping me to think about the whole experience of Christian life and how important the act of "remembering" is. So many of the virtues and vices cited earlier in constructing a spirituality of administration or thinking of the necessary "habits of the heart" for a Christian perspective on administrative service have to do with "remembering." Remembering the fundamental Gospel mission of the institutions we serve. Remembering that the everyday tasks of administration can also be expressions of our Christian vocation to serve. Remembering that the people with whom we work are also noble human beings and children of God. Remembering that the ultimate purpose of our lives as followers of Jesus and the very purpose of the institutions in which we serve are to give life and meaning to God's people.

These acts of remembering, animated by the power of God's Spirit, can enable us to see that administrative service is indeed a gift to the Church and a genuine expression of our call to discipleship.

Select Bibliography

Achtemeier, Paul J. *1 Peter*. Heremeneia. Minneapolis, MN: Fortress, 1996.

Bahls, Steven C. *Shared Governance in Times of Change: A Practical Guide for Universities and Colleges*. Washington, DC. AGB Press, 2014.

Balch, David, and Carolyn Osiek. *Early Christian Families in Context: An Interdisciplinary Dialogue*. Grand Rapids, MI: Eerdmans, 2003.

Benefiel, Margaret. *Soul at Work: Spiritual Leadership in Organizations*. New York: Seabury Press, 2005.

Bockmuehl, Markus. *Simon Peter in Scripture and Memory: The New Testament Apostle in the Early Church*. Grand Rapids, MI: Baker Academic, 2012.

Bonhoeffer, Dietrich. *Life Together: A Discussion of Christian Fellowship*. New York: HarperCollins, 1954.

Briones, D. E. *Paul's Financial Policy*. New York: T & T Clark, 2013.

Conway, Daniel, Anita Rook, and Daniel A. Schipp. *The Reluctant Steward: A Report and Commentary on the Stewardship and Development Study*. Indianapolis, IN and St. Meinrad, IN: Christian Theological Seminary and St. Meinrad Seminary, 1992.

Conway, Daniel. *The Reluctant Steward Revisited: Preparing Pastors for Administrative and Financial Duties: A Report and Commentary on a Study Conducted by St. Meinrad School of Theology with funding from Lilly Endowment Inc.* St. Meinrad, IN: St. Meinrad School of Theology, 2002.

Covey, Stephen. *The 7 Habits of Highly Effective People: Powerful Lessons in Personal Change*. New York: Simon and Schuster, 2004.

Dayton, Howard L. Jr. *Your Money Counts: The Biblical Guide to Earning, Spending, Saving, Investing, Giving, and Getting Out of Debt.* Carol Stream IL: Tyndale House Publishers, 1997.

Dunn, James D. G. *The Epistles to the Colossians and to Philemon.* New International Greek Testament Commentary. Grand Rapids, MI: Eerdmans, 1996.

Elliott, John H. *I Peter.* The Anchor Bible Yale Commentaries. Volume 37 B. New York: Doubleday, 2000.

Fox, Zeni, and Regina Bechtle, eds. *Called & Chosen: Toward a Spirituality for Lay Leaders.* Lanham, MD: Rowan and Littlefield, 2005.

Francis. *Evangelii Gaudium* (The Joy of the Gospel). Washington, DC: United States Conference of Catholic Bishops, 2013.

———. "Presentation of the Christmas Greetings to the Roman Curia. Address of His Holiness Pope Francis, Monday, December 22, 2014." https://w2.vatican.va/content/francesco /en/speeches/2014/december/documents/papa-francesco _20141222_curia-romana.html.

Garrido, Ann M. *Redeeming Administration: 12 Spiritual Habits for Catholic Leaders in Parishes, Schools, Religious Communities, and Other Institutions.* Notre Dame, IN: Ave Maria Press, 2013.

———. "More Than a Desk Job: The Spirituality of Administration." *America* 201, no. 1 (July 6, 2009): 22–23.

Greenleaf, R. K. *The Servant as Leader.* Westfield, IN: The Robert K. Greenleaf Center, 1991.

———. *The Power of Servant Leadership.* Edited by Larry C. Spears. San Francisco: Berrett-Koehler, 1998.

Grudem, Wayne. *Business for the Glory of God: The Bible's Teaching on the Moral Goodness of Business.* Wheaton, IL: Crossway Books, 2003.

Heifitz, Ronald A. *The Practice of Adaptive Leadership: Tools and Tactics for Changing Your Organization and the World.* Cambridge, MA: Harvard Business Press, 2009.

Heifitz, Ronald A., and Marty Linsky. *Leadership on the Line: Staying Alive through the Dangers of Leading.* Cambridge, MA: Harvard Business School Press, 2002.

Hengel, Martin. *The Charismatic Leader and His Followers*. New York: Crossroads, 1981.

Jewett, Robert. *Romans*. Hermeneia. Minneapolis, MN: Fortress Press, 2007.

Juel, Donald. *Messiah and Temple*. SBL Dissertation Series. Missoula, MO: Scholars Press, 1977.

Keck, David. *Forgetting Whose We Are: Alzheimer's Disease and the Love of God*. Nashville, TN: Abingdon, 1996.

Lewis, G. Douglass, and Lovett H. Weems Jr., eds. *A Handbook for Seminary Presidents*. Grand Rapids, MI: Eerdmans, 2006.

Lencioni, Patrick. *The Five Dysfunctions of a Team: A Leadership Fable*. San Francisco: Jossey-Bass, 2002.

Lynn, Robert W. "Faith and Money: The Need for a New Understanding of Stewardship." In *The Reluctant Steward: A Report and Commentary on the Stewardship and Development Study*, edited by Daniel Conway, Anita Rook, and Daniel A. Schipp, p. 31. Indianapolis, IN and St. Meinrad, IN: Christian Theological Seminary and St. Meinrad Seminary, 1992.

MacDonald, Margaret Y. *Colossians and Ephesians*. Sacra Pagina. Collegeville MN: Liturgical Press, 2000.

———. *The Power of Children: The Construction of Christian Families in the Greco-Roman World*. Waco, TX: Baylor University Press, 2014.

McKnight, Scot. "Collection for the Saints." In *Dictionary of Paul and His Letters*, edited by Gerald F. Hawthorne, Ralph P. Martin, and Daniel G. Reid, pp. 143–47. Downers Grove, IL: InterVarsity Press, 1993.

McLaughlin, Thomas A. *Streetsmart: Basics for Nonprofit Managers*. 3rd ed. Hoboken, NJ: John Wiley and Sons, 2009.

Marshall, I. Howard. *The Pastoral Epistles*. ICC. Edinburgh: T & T Clark, 1999.

Nouwen, Henri. *A Spirituality of Fundraising*. Nashville, TN: Upper Room Books, 2010.

Ogereau, Julien M. "Paul's κοινωνία with the Philippians: Societas as a Missionary Funding Strategy." *New Testament Studies* 60 (2014): 360–78.

O'Loughlin, Thomas. *The Didache: A Window on the Earliest Christians.* Grand Rapids, MI: Baker Academic, 2010.

Ouellette, Helen, and Barbara Wheeler. "Two Patterns of Good Governance." *In Trust* 26, no. 2 (Spring 2015): 19–23.

Perrin, Nicholas. *Jesus the Temple.* Grand Rapids, MI: Baker Academic, 2010.

Putnam, Robert. *Bowling Alone: The Collapse and Revival of American Community.* New York: Simon and Schuster, 2000.

Ruger, Anthony, John Canary, and Steven Land. "The President's Role in Financial Management." In *A Handbook for Seminary Residents.* Edited by C. Douglass Lewis and Lovett H. Weems Jr. Grand Rapids, MI: Eerdmans, 2006.

Second Vatican Council. *Gaudium et Spes* (The Pastoral Constitution on the Church in the Modern World). In *Vatican Council II: The Conciliar and Postconciliar Documents.* Translated by Austin Flannery. Collegeville MN: Liturgical Press, 2014.

Senior, Donald. "Financial Support for the Church and Our Biblical Heritage." *New Theology Review* 9 (1996): 38–51.

———. "'Speaking the Very Words of God': New Testament Perspectives on the Characteristics of Christian Speech." In *Between Experience and Interpretation: Engaging the Writings of the New Testament,* edited by Mary F. Foskett and Wes Allen, pp. 35–52. Nashville, TN: Abingdon, 2008.

Senior, Donald, and Daniel Harrington. *1 Peter Jude and 2 Peter.* Sacra Pagina. Collegeville, MN: Liturgical Press, 2003.

Stepansky, R. J. *Thoughts on Leadership from a Higher Level: Leadership Lessons from the Bible.* Suwanee, GA: Deeper Calling Media, 2015. E-book.

Stewart, Alistair C. *The Original Bishops: Office and Order in the First Christian Communities* Grand Rapids, MI: Eerdmans, 2014.

Tiede, David. "Faculty Powers in Shared Governance." *Theological Education* 44 (2009): 29–37.

United States Conference of Catholic Bishops. *Stewardship: A Disciple's Response.* Washington, DC: USCCB, 1997.

Wheeler, Barbara G. "Effective Leadership for Theological Schools." *In Trust* 26, no. 1 (New Year 2015).

Wheeler, Barbara G., G. Douglass Lewis, Sharon L. Miller, Anthony T. Ruger, and David L. Tiede. *Leadership that Works: A Study of Theological School Presidents.* Auburn Studies 15 (December 2010).

Williams, Oliver F., ed. *Religion, Business, and Spirituality.* Notre Dame, IN: University of Notre Dame Press, 2003.

Zietlow, John. *Financial Management for Nonprofit Organizations: Policies and Practices.* Hoboken, NJ: John Wiley and Sons, 2007.

Index